Celebrating Sunday
for Catholic Families
2023–2024

Mary Heinrich

LTP
LITURGY
TRAINING
PUBLICATIONS

Nihil Obstat
Deacon David Keene, PHD
Chancellor
Archdiocese of Chicago
September 6, 2022

Imprimatur
Most Rev. Robert G. Casey
Vicar General
Archdiocese of Chicago
September 6, 2022

The *Nihil Obstat* and *Imprimatur* are declarations that the material is free from doctrinal or moral error, and thus is granted permission to publish in accordance with c. 827. No legal responsibility is assumed by the grant of this permission. No implication is contained herein that those who have granted the *Nihil Obstat* and *Imprimatur* agree with the content, opinions, or statements expressed.

Celebrating Sunday for Catholic Families 2023–2024 © 2023 Archdiocese of Chicago: Liturgy Training Publications, 3949 South Racine Avenue, Chicago, IL 60609; 800-933-1800; fax: 800-933-7094; email: orders@ltp.org; website: www.LTP.org. All rights reserved.

This book was edited by Rachel Espinoza. Víctor R. Pérez was the production editor, Anna Manhart was the designer, and Kari Nicholls was the production artist.

Cover art © William Hernandez.

Printed in the United States of America

ISBN 978-1-61671-698-1

CSCF24

"You shall love the Lord your God with all your heart and with all your soul and with all your might. Keep these words that I am commanding you today in your heart. Recite them to your children and talk about them when you are at home and when you are away, when you lie down and when you rise."

Deuteronomy 6:5–7, NRSVUE

Contents

How to Use

Celebrating Sunday for Catholic Families

This small weekly guide draws on the Gospel for each Sunday and Holyday for the coming year. It is intended to help parents engage their children with the Mass and deepen their appreciation of the richness of their faith life. So often, going to Mass becomes a weekly event that begins and ends at the church door. The brief reflection on an excerpt from the Gospel is intended to spark your thinking about the Scripture that will lead to conversation with your family before and after Mass. Suggestions for questions and conversation starters are provided, as well as some practice or practical way to carry this reflection into the life of the family. Keep in mind, however, that sometimes you may have other needs, concerns, or ideas that are more relevant to your home life at that moment. If so, engage your children with those.

Note that very young children are able to enter into the liturgy through their senses. Singing the hymns, calling their attention to the changing colors of the liturgical seasons, and sitting where they can observe the gestures of the Mass are all ways to form them in the faith. Always remember, as the rite of baptism proclaims, you, as parents, are your children's first and most important teachers. We hope that this book will enrich your family's life of faith.

September 10, 2023

Twenty-Third Sunday in Ordinary Time

Hearing the Word
Matthew 18:15–20

In the name of the Father, and of the Son, and of the Holy Spirit.

Jesus said to his disciples: "If your brother sins against you, go and tell him his fault between you and him alone. If he listens to you, you have won over your brother. If he does not listen, take one or two others along with you, so that 'every fact may be established on the testimony of two or three witnesses.' If he refuses to listen to them, tell the church. If he refuses to listen even to the church, then treat him as you would a Gentile or a tax collector. Amen, I say to you, whatever you bind on earth shall be bound in heaven, and whatever you loose on earth shall be loosed in heaven. Again, amen, I say to you, if two of you agree on earth about anything for which they are to pray, it shall be granted to them by my heavenly Father. For where two or three are gathered together in my name, there am I in the midst of them."

Reflecting on the Word

In today's Gospel, Jesus prescribes a method to handle disagreements, and the prescription escalates, depending on how corrections are received by the party at fault. When faced with relational challenges, it is good to center ourselves in quiet and to reflect on these words of Jesus for how to resolve conflicts. How might the practice of listening for God's voice in silence help us in our day-to-day interactions with others, especially with those who do not see eye-to-eye with us?

......ON THE WAY TO MASS

At Mass, we know that Jesus Christ is present in both Word and sacrament. How do we recognize him in the lives and hearts of those in our community? What makes it difficult to see Christ in others?

ON THE WAY HOME FROM MASS ......

How can family members listen better or practice patience with one another when frustrations arise?

Living the Word

Recognizing Christ, especially in those with whom we disagree, involves listening. We need to practice being silent so that we can listen to God. Have your children practice being still without distractions, even if just for a minute. Ask them, "Can you keep your hands and arms silent? Your feet and legs silent? Your eyes closed and mouth silent? In the silence, what did you hear in your heart?"

September 17, 2023

Twenty-Fourth Sunday in Ordinary Time

Hearing the Word

Matthew 18:21–22

In the name of the Father, and of the Son, and of the Holy Spirit.

Peter approached Jesus and asked him, "Lord, if my brother sins against me, how often must I forgive? As many as seven times?" Jesus answered, "I say to you, not seven times but seventy-seven times."

Reflecting on the Word

Peter asks Jesus about a topic that is as challenging for us as it was for him: forgiveness! Whether we are six or sixty years old, we also have questions about forgiveness: How do we feel when people hurt us? Do we still love them? Do we carry anger in our heart? Do we try to hurt them back? Do we forgive them right away? Does it still hurt even after we forgive them? Jesus' words challenge us to choose forgiveness over and over again, and not let the questions that arise in our hearts keep us stuck in unforgiveness.

......ON THE WAY TO MASS

The Mass is one great prayer made up of many prayers. Let us listen for the words *sorry, forgive, mercy,* and *peace* in today's liturgy. Are they words proclaimed by the priest, spoken by the assembly (us), or both?

ON THE WAY HOME FROM MASS ......

How can we bring our experience of conflict to Jesus and ask him for help in our time of need?

Living the Word

Each night this week, talk with your children about the moments during the day that they either asked someone for forgiveness or forgave someone. Did they ask Jesus for forgiveness? How do they feel after forgiving someone? How does it feel to know that Jesus forgives them?

September 24, 2023

Twenty-Fifth Sunday in Ordinary Time

Hearing the Word

Matthew 20:8–15

In the name of the Father, and of the Son, and of the Holy Spirit.

"When it was evening the owner of the vineyard said to his foreman, 'Summon the laborers and give them their pay, beginning with the last and ending with the first.' When those who had started about five o'clock came, each received the usual daily wage. So when the first came, they thought that they would receive more, but each of them also got the usual wage. And on receiving it they grumbled against the land-owner, saying, 'These last ones worked only one hour, and you have made them equal to us, who bore the day's burden and the heat.' He said to one of them in reply, 'My friend, I am not cheating you. Did you not agree with me for the usual daily wage? Take what is yours and go . . . Are you envious because I am generous?'"

Reflecting on the Word

God invites all to be workers in building the kingdom, but he calls people, and they answer at different times. While it may not seem fair that the last to be called is given the same reward as the first, we recognize that God's ways are not our ways. Jesus reminds us that God gives love and grace freely to everyone, and that all his children are equally important to him, no matter when they answer his call.

. . . . . . ON THE WAY TO MASS

Have you ever felt jealous of someone for having more than you do? Why?

ON THE WAY HOME FROM MASS . . . . . .

Why do you think the owner of the vineyard gave the workers who arrived late in the day the same pay as those who arrived early in the day? What does this tell us about God's generosity?

Living the Word

Today's Gospel reminds us that we are to imitate God's own generosity with others. Sadly, we know that in our world, not everyone has everything they need to flourish. Discuss with your family how some people do not have enough food or a place to live, or do not have adequate wages to provide for their family's needs. Decide on one small action that your family can do toward eradicating those injustices.

October 1, 2023

Twenty-Sixth Sunday in Ordinary Time

Hearing the Word

Matthew 21:28–32

In the name of the Father, and of the Son, and of the Holy Spirit.

Jesus said to the chief priests and elders of the people: "What is your opinion? A man had two sons. He came to the first and said, 'Son, go out and work in the vineyard today.' He said in reply, 'I will not,' but afterwards changed his mind and went. The man came to the other son and gave the same order. He said in reply, 'Yes, sir,' but did not go. Which of the two did his father's will?" They answered, "The first." Jesus said to them, "Amen, I say to you, tax collectors and prostitutes are entering the kingdom of God before you. When John came to you in the way of righteousness, you did not believe him; but tax collectors and prostitutes did. Yet even when you saw that, you did not later change your minds and believe him."

Reflecting on the Word

It is easy to see ourselves as either the first or the second son in today's Gospel. Sometimes we are the first son—we initially refuse God and ignore his will for us, but through prayer and discernment, we have a change of heart. At other times, we are the second son, and have every intention of responding to what God calls us to do but get distracted or do not follow through. How is the Lord calling us to bring our words and our actions into alignment this week?

......ON THE WAY TO MASS

At Mass today we will pray the Our Father, saying, "Thy kingdom come, thy will be done." Ask your children to think about God's will. What does that mean?

ON THE WAY HOME FROM MASS ......

Ask your children whether actions speak louder than words. How?

Living the Word

At home, look up Scripture verses in which Jesus speaks about following the Father's will: the Agony in the Garden: Matthew 26:39, 42; Luke 22:42; the True Disciple: Matthew 7:21; and Jesus and His Family: Mark 3:35. Discuss: How do we know God's will for us? How is Jesus a model for us in discerning God's will and following it, even if sometimes it is hard to? Have your children make and decorate a prayer card with the words "thy kingdom come, thy will be done" from the Our Father. Place this card somewhere you will see it as a reminder to follow God's will.

October 8, 2023

Twenty-Seventh Sunday in Ordinary Time

Hearing the Word

Matthew 21:33–35, 37, 39–41

In the name of the Father, and of the Son, and of the Holy Spirit.

Jesus said to the chief priests and the elders of the people: "Hear another parable. There was a landowner who planted a vineyard, put a hedge around it, dug a wine press in it, and built a tower. Then he leased it to tenants and went on a journey. When vintage time drew near, he sent his servants to the tenants to obtain his produce. But the tenants seized the servants and one they beat, another they killed, and a third they stoned. Finally, he sent his son to them, thinking, 'They will respect my son.' They seized him, threw him out of the vineyard, and killed him. What will the owner of the vineyard do to those tenants when he comes?" They answered him, "He will put those wretched men to a wretched death and lease his vineyard to other tenants who will give him the produce at the proper times."

Reflecting on the Word

We are all workers in God's vineyard. There are many people who are a part of God's plan and who proclaim his Word among us—from the prophets, the disciples, the evangelists, the pope, our parish priests, catechists, and even members of our family. How might we be more receptive to God and his messengers? How are we each called to be proclaimers and listeners to his Word?

•••••• ON THE WAY TO MASS

Have you ever been put in charge of something, or been asked to do a task for someone else? How did it go?

ON THE WAY HOME FROM MASS ••••••

A tenant *is one* who works the land *but* does not own it. How can we be a good tenant in the vineyard this week?

Living the Word

The vineyard's grapevines produce grapes, a fruit that many enjoy eating. As workers in God's vineyard, what type of "fruit" are we called to produce? If we are full of the light of the risen Christ, how will it show on the outside? Let us think of ways we can show others that we belong to God. Have your children make a list to post in a place at home where everyone will be able to see it. How will you and your family accomplish items on the list this week, this month, this year?

October 15, 2023

Twenty-Eighth Sunday in Ordinary Time

Hearing the Word

Matthew 22:1–10

In the name of the Father, and of the Son, and of the Holy Spirit.

Jesus again in reply spoke to the chief priests and elders of the people in parables, saying, "The kingdom of heaven may be likened to a king who gave a wedding feast for his son. He dispatched his servants to summon the invited guests to the feast, but they refused to come. A second time he sent other servants, saying, 'Tell those invited: "Behold, I have prepared my banquet, my calves and fattened cattle are killed, and everything is ready; come to the feast."' Some ignored the invitation and went away, one to his farm, another to his business. The rest laid hold of his servants, mistreated them, and killed them. The king was enraged and sent his troops, destroyed those murderers, and burned their city. Then he said to his servants, 'The feast is ready, but those who were invited were not worthy to come. Go out, therefore, into the main roads and invite to the feast whomever you find.' The servants went out into the streets and gathered all they found, bad and good alike, and the hall was filled with guests."

Reflecting on the Word

Have you ever had to prepare invitations for a birthday party or other family event? We send out invitations and hope that those invited will come, because we look forward to gathering with those we love. Today's Gospel reminds us that the Lord prepares a banquet for us and has invited us to join the feast! Just as we desire to gather with loved ones, the Lord eagerly awaits our coming to him. Ask him to help you respond to his invitation with joy.

······ ON THE WAY TO MASS

What are some things that get in the way of seeing God's invitation in our lives? What worries take our time and attention away from God?

ON THE WAY HOME FROM MASS ······

Jesus preaches often about the kingdom of God and what life will be like there. Today's Gospel image of the kingdom is a wedding feast. How do you imagine the kingdom of God? What is it like?

Living the Word

To receive an invitation is special. How have we been invited into a relationship with God? Who are the people who have been the messengers of this generous invitation? Make a list of the people whose voices and actions invite us to draw closer to God. Write thank-you notes or call them on the phone to thank them for being a witness to the kingdom.

October 22, 2023

Twenty-Ninth Sunday in Ordinary Time

Hearing the Word

Matthew 22:15–21

In the name of the Father, and of the Son, and of the Holy Spirit.

The Pharisees went off and plotted how they might entrap Jesus in speech. They sent their disciples to him, with the Herodians, saying, "Teacher, we know that you are a truthful man and that you teach the way of God in accordance with the truth. And you are not concerned with anyone's opinion, for you do not regard a person's status. Tell us, then, what is your opinion: Is it lawful to pay the census tax to Caesar or not?" Knowing their malice, Jesus said, "Why are you testing me, you hypocrites? Show me the coin that pays the census tax." Then they handed him the Roman coin. He said to them, "Whose image is this and whose inscription?" They replied, "Caesar's." At that he said to them, "Then repay to Caesar what belongs to Caesar and to God what belongs to God."

Reflecting on the Word

At the center of this story lies two questions: "What do we owe to God?" and "Does what we owe to God ever put us at odds with civil authority?" The gift owed to God is far more valuable than money and rises above anything demanded of us by the government. God wants our hearts! To give God what is God's is to give him our worries, our struggles, and our pains, as well as our joy and our love. How will you give God more of your heart this week?

......ON THE WAY TO MASS

Ask your children to think about the following questions: "What is God asking me to give to him today? What do we offer to him at Mass?"

ON THE WAY HOME FROM MASS ......

Jesus tells the Pharisees to "repay to Caesar what belongs to Caesar and to God what belongs to God." What do you think it means to belong to God?

Living the Word

Prayer is an important way that we give to God what is God's. In prayer, we give God our hearts. Make an inventory of all the times and ways we pray during the day. As a family, discuss how you can spend more time with God in prayer. Are there new times that you could incorporate prayer into your life together? Are there new ways of praying you want to explore? Add one time or one new way of praying to your life this week.

October 29, 2023

Thirtieth Sunday in Ordinary Time

Hearing the Word

Matthew 22:34–40

In the name of the Father, and of the Son, and of the Holy Spirit.

When the Pharisees heard that Jesus had silenced the Sadducees, they gathered together, and one of them, a scholar of the law tested him by asking, "Teacher, which commandment in the law is the greatest?" He said to him, "You shall love the Lord, your God, with all your heart, with all your soul, and with all your mind. This is the greatest and the first commandment. The second is like it: You shall love your neighbor as yourself. The whole law and the prophets depend on these two commandments."

Reflecting on the Word

When the Pharisees question Jesus about the greatest commandment, Jesus tells them to love God with all your heart, mind, soul, and love your neighbor as yourself. As parents, we do so much to show love to our family members, but we often forget that an important part of the commandment is love of self. How often do we show love to ourselves? Do we eat good food and get plenty of rest? What are other ways that we can we love ourselves?

......ON THE WAY TO MASS

Ask your children, "How do we love God with all that we are?"

ON THE WAY HOME FROM MASS ......

Ask your children, "Is it easier to love God or to love ourselves?"

Living the Word

As a family, think about how you can follow this twofold commandment, with particular focus on loving your neighbor this week. Discuss together: What is an expression of love that could be offered to a neighbor? Decide on one act of kindness you could do, from something as simple as offering a smile and saying hello to a neighbor on a walk through your neighborhood, to sharing your cooking or baking skills with someone on your block. Then be sure to work together to put your thoughts into action in the week ahead.

November 1, 2023

Solemnity of All Saints

Hearing the Word
Matthew 5:3–12a

In the name of the Father, and of the Son, and of the Holy Spirit.

[Jesus said:] "Blessed are the poor in spirit, / for theirs is the Kingdom of heaven. / Blessed are they who mourn, / for they will be comforted. / Blessed are the meek, / for they will inherit the land. / Blessed are they who hunger and thirst for righteousness, / for they will be satisfied. / Blessed are the merciful, / for they will be shown mercy. / Blessed are the clean of heart, / for they will see God. / Blessed are the peacemakers, / for they will be called children of God. / Blessed are they who are persecuted for the sake of righteousness, / for theirs is the Kingdom of heaven. / Blessed are you when they insult you and persecute you / and utter every kind of evil against you falsely because of me. / Rejoice and be glad, / for your reward will be great in heaven."

Reflecting on the Word

There is a great deal of sadness and sorrow in the world. We see it in the news, in the workplace, and in our everyday lives. The Beatitudes remind us that God offers an abundance of blessings to those who are hurting or who find themselves in humble circumstances. In God's kingdom, the poor are blessed, the meek and lowly inherit the earth, and the hungry are filled. Through these promises, God reminds us that we are never abandoned and that he will help us through any difficulty we may face.

......ON THE WAY TO MASS

The Mass is where we receive many blessings. Ask your children to watch and listen for the moments when the priest prays a prayer of blessing. Are there certain words or actions you recognize within these blessings?

ON THE WAY HOME FROM MASS ......

The word *blessed* appears in today's Gospel nine times. What does it mean to be blessed? How does God show his love through these blessings?

Living the Word

The Beatitudes tell us that we have been blessed. Think about some of the people mentioned in the Beatitudes. How can you bring God's blessing to them? For example, for those who hunger, can you make sack lunches to donate to those in need? For those who mourn, can you send a sympathy card or offer prayers or practical support (meals, help with chores, and so on)? Choose one action and do it together as a family this week.

November 5, 2023

Thirty-First Sunday in Ordinary Time

Hearing the Word

Matthew 23:1–12

In the name of the Father, and of the Son, and of the Holy Spirit.

Jesus spoke to the crowds and to his disciples, saying, "The scribes and the Pharisees have taken their seat on the chair of Moses. Therefore, do and observe all things whatsoever they tell you, but do not follow their example. For they preach but they do not practice. They tie up heavy burdens hard to carry and lay them on people's shoulders, but they will not lift a finger to move them. All their works are performed to be seen. They widen their phylacteries and lengthen their tassels. They love places of honor at banquets, seats of honor in synagogues, greetings in marketplaces, and the salutation 'Rabbi.' As for you, do not be called 'Rabbi.' You have but one teacher, and you are all brothers. Call no one on earth your father; you have but one Father in heaven. Do not be called 'Master'; you have but one master, the Christ. The greatest among you must be your servant. Whoever exalts himself will be humbled; but whoever humbles himself will be exalted."

Reflecting on the Word

In today's Gospel, the scribes and Pharisees are concerned with status, position, and keeping up appearances, but Jesus reminds his followers that to be a disciple means to be a servant. Jesus tells us, "The greatest among you must be your servant. Whoever exalts himself will be humbled; but whoever humbles himself will be exalted." We should not seek to honor ourselves but give all honor and glory to God by humbly serving the needs of others. What would the world look like if everyone lived this aspect of the Gospel message?

• • • • • • ON THE WAY TO MASS

Jesus invites us to love as he loves, and to serve as he serves. What are some ways we can care for or help others?

ON THE WAY HOME FROM MASS • • • • • •

Who is God calling us to serve today? How is God's love going to be shared with others through our family today? When we serve others with a humble heart, we give all glory and honor to God!

Living the Word

The saints are men, women, and children who have chosen to be servants of God. When we read about their lives, we see examples of how to be holy and how to serve others. Choose a saint (any saint, or perhaps the patron saint of your parish, if applicable) and read about his or her life. Discuss how that saint chose to serve God, and what lessons your family can take from their example.

November 12, 2023

Thirty-Second Sunday in Ordinary Time

Hearing the Word

Matthew 25:1–13

In the name of the Father, and of the Son, and of the Holy Spirit.

Jesus told his disciples this parable: "The kingdom of heaven will be like ten virgins who took their lamps and went out to meet the bridegroom. Five of them were foolish and five were wise. The foolish ones, when taking their lamps, brought no oil with them, but the wise brought flasks of oil with their lamps. Since the bridegroom was long delayed, they all became drowsy and fell asleep. At midnight, there was a cry, 'Behold, the bridegroom! Come out to meet him!' Then all those virgins got up and trimmed their lamps. The foolish ones said to the wise, 'Give us some of your oil, for our lamps are going out.' But the wise ones replied, 'No, for there may not be enough for us and you. Go instead to the merchants and buy some for yourselves.' While they went off to buy it, the bridegroom came and those who were ready went into the wedding feast with him. Then the door was locked. Afterwards the other virgins came and said, 'Lord, Lord, open the door for us!' But he said in reply, 'Amen, I say to you, I do not know you.' Therefore, stay awake, for you know neither the day nor the hour."

Reflecting on the Word

As parents, we often prepare for a myriad of family gatherings, taking care of the arrangements and putting every detail in order. Preparation is essential, whether we are getting ready for a birthday party, a family reunion, or a wedding feast as in today's Gospel. At the time of Jesus, oil was used in clay lamps to provide light. Five of the young women bring extra oil, so that their lamps would remain lit, while five foolish young women are unprepared and do not have the necessary oil. They find themselves in darkness, locked outside of the wedding feast. We are called to be diligent in our spiritual preparation, so that we may walk in the light.

•••••• ON THE WAY TO MASS

Ask your children, "How can we be prepared to receive Jesus when he comes to us?" Think about the ways you prepare yourself for Mass and to receive Jesus in the Eucharist. What else can you do to prepare your hearts for Mass?

ON THE WAY HOME FROM MASS ••••••

What do you think Jesus meant when he talked about keeping our light burning? How can we make sure we are ready to meet him when he comes?

Living the Word

Recall your children's response to the question of how we can keep our light burning. Invite them to choose one idea to live out in the week ahead, so that you are prepared to welcome the Bridegroom when he comes.

Thirty-Third Sunday in Ordinary Time

Hearing the Word

Matthew 25:14–15, 19–21

In the name of the Father, and of the Son, and of the Holy Spirit.

Jesus told his disciples this parable: "A man going on a journey called in his servants and entrusted his possessions to them. To one he gave five talents; to another, two; to a third, one—to each according to his ability. Then he went away.

"After a long time the master of those servants came back and settled accounts with them. The one who had received five talents came forward bringing the additional five. He said, 'Master, you gave me five talents. See, I have made five more.' His master said to him, 'Well done, my good and faithful servant. Since you were faithful in small matters, I will give you great responsibilities. Come, share your master's joy.'"

Reflecting on the Word

We are often the ones who first notice new talents showing up in our children's lives. As parents, it's our job to point these out and to help our children put them to use. As they attempt to use their God-given gifts, our children may be afraid to try new things. We can encourage them to take new risks by entrusting them with greater levels of responsibility as they grow, demonstrating our faith in their abilities and by offering support throughout the process. Finally, we all long to hear "well done, my good and faithful servant." Be sure to offer regular words of affirmation as you encourage your children to use their gifts.

•••••• ON THE WAY TO MASS

Ask your children, "Why do people have such different gifts? What do you think God wants you to do with your gifts?"

ON THE WAY HOME FROM MASS ••••••

What happens if we do not use our gifts? What happens when we do use our gifts? To whom do these talents belong?

Living the Word

Write a list of talents or gifts seen in each family member. Read the list aloud, affirming each person, perhaps offering examples of how they demonstrate that gift in daily life. Invite each family member to consider which gift, skill, or talent they most enjoy and how that gift may be used to build the kingdom of God.

November 26, 2023

Solemnity of Our Lord Jesus Christ, King of the Universe

Hearing the Word

Matthew 25:31–36

In the name of the Father, and of the Son, and of the Holy Spirit.

Jesus said to his disciples: "When the Son of Man comes in his glory, and all the angels with him, he will sit upon his glorious throne, and all the nations will be assembled before him. And he will separate them one from another, as a shepherd separates the sheep from the goats. He will place the sheep on his right and the goats on his left. Then the king will say to those on his right, 'Come, you who are blessed by my Father. Inherit the kingdom prepared for you from the foundation of the world. For I was hungry and you gave me food, I was thirsty and you gave me drink, a stranger and you welcomed me, naked and you clothed me, ill and you cared for me, in prison and you visited me.'"

Reflecting on the Word

We don't have to look very far for opportunities to care for the least of these! We serve the hungry and thirsty every time we make a peanut butter and jelly sandwich for, or offer a glass of water, Kool-Aid, or milk to our children. We provide our children with shelter in our wombs, then in our arms, and clothe them with diapers and clothing (which brings its own joy of endless laundry). We recognize the gifts of the youngest and smallest, chasing after older siblings—wanting to join in, but feeling imprisoned in their littleness. Whenever we act with mercy toward the most vulnerable among us, we show mercy to Jesus.

······ ON THE WAY TO MASS

Ask your children, "When was the last time you saw someone who was in need? Hungry? Thirsty? A Stranger? Naked? Sick? Imprisoned?" What did you do to respond? What might you do next time?

ON THE WAY HOME FROM MASS ······

Who are the "least among us" and why should we show them kindness?

Living the Word

We are called to be intentional in our acts of kindness for the least among us. How can your family live the Corporal Works of Mercy this week? Select one work of mercy and discern how you will show God's love and kindness this week.

December 3, 2023

First Sunday of Advent

Hearing the Word

Mark 13:33–37

In the name of the Father, and of the Son, and of the Holy Spirit.

Jesus said to his disciples: "Be watchful! Be alert! You do not know when the time will come. It is like a man traveling abroad. He leaves home and places his servants in charge, each with his own work, and orders the gatekeeper to be on the watch. Watch, therefore; you do not know when the lord of the house is coming, whether in the evening, or at midnight, or at cockcrow, or in the morning. May he not come suddenly and find you sleeping. What I say to you, I say to all: 'Watch!'"

Reflecting on the Word

As parents, we have stayed awake with a late-night feeding, with a sick child, or waiting for a teenager to return home from an evening out with friends. Even when we are tired or weary, we are alert to the needs of our children. We are called to practice the same kind of alertness in our spiritual life. As God's servants, he has given us responsibility, a particular work to do. We know that he is coming. How do we keep our eyes, and our hearts open to his return, so that we are ready when he comes?

......ON THE WAY TO MASS

To be alert means to be wide awake. How can watch for Jesus today?

ON THE WAY HOME FROM MASS ......

How have we been awakened to all the ways Jesus comes to us?

Living the Word

Create a "Be Watchful! Be Alert! Jesus Is Coming!" sign and list every time a family member is aware of how or when Jesus has come to your home or your heart. It may be a moment on the school playground, at the grocery store, or around the kitchen table. Note the date, the time, and a brief description to help you track how often we are aware of Jesus' presence in our daily lives. The goal is that through this exercise, your family will become more attuned to the many occasions God is present in daily life.

December 8, 2023

Solemnity of the Immaculate Conception of the Blessed Virgin Mary

Hearing the Word

Luke 1:26–31, 34–38b

In the name of the Father, and of the Son, and of the Holy Spirit.

The angel Gabriel was sent from God to a town of Galilee called Nazareth, to a virgin betrothed to a man named Joseph, of the house of David, and the virgin's name was Mary. And coming to her, he said, "Hail, full of grace! The Lord is with you." But she was greatly troubled at what was said and pondered what sort of greeting this might be. Then the angel said to her, "Do not be afraid, Mary, for you have found favor with God. Behold, you will conceive in your womb and bear a son, and you shall name him Jesus." But Mary said to the angel, "How can this be, since I have no relations with a man?" And the angel said to her in reply, "The Holy Spirit will come upon you, and the power of the Most High will overshadow you. Therefore the child to be born will be called holy, the Son of God. And behold, Elizabeth, your relative, has also conceived a son in her old age, and this is the sixth month for her who was called barren; for nothing will be impossible for God." Mary said, "Behold, I am the handmaid of the Lord. May it be done to me according to your word."

Reflecting on the Word

Like all of Israel, Mary was waiting for the Messiah. When the angel Gabriel visited Mary in her home in Nazareth, he gave her some amazing news that she was being called to be the mother of the Lord! We may wonder, what made this young girl so special? She was lowly, not rich; nor was she proud or famous. Yet God chose her for this task, and she responded to God's invitation. After Gabriel's visit, Mary waits for the arrival of her Son. How can we join Mary in her waiting?

......ON THE WAY TO MASS

Let us listen for the Holy Spirit in today's Gospel. What is the work of the Holy Spirit? What does the Holy Spirit reveal to us about this child? this mother?

ON THE WAY HOME FROM MASS ......

Mary told the angel that she was a handmaid of the Lord. What does it mean to be a handmaid of the Lord? How is each member of our household called to serve the Lord? Is the Holy Spirit connected to our service to God?

Living the Word

The angel greeted Mary with words that may be familiar to us: "Hail, full of grace! The Lord is with you!" Where have we heard these words before? Write these lovely words on a prayer card or have your children draw an image of the angel Gabriel coming to Mary to place on the prayer table. Each night this week, read the prayer card or pray the Hail Mary prayer as a family, and think deeply about the angel's words to Mary.

December 10, 2023

Second Sunday of Advent

Hearing the Word
Mark 1:1–5, 7–8

In the name of the Father, and of the Son, and of the Holy Spirit.

The beginning of the gospel of Jesus Christ the Son of God.

As it is written in Isaiah the prophet: / *Behold, I am sending my messenger ahead of you; / he will prepare your way. / A voice of one crying out in the desert: / "Prepare the way of the Lord, / make straight his paths."* / John the Baptist appeared in the desert proclaiming a baptism of repentance for the forgiveness of sins. People of the whole Judean countryside and all the inhabitants of Jerusalem were going out to him and were being baptized by him in the Jordan River as they acknowledged their sins. And this is what he proclaimed: "One mightier than I is coming after me. I am not worthy to stoop and loosen the thongs of his sandals. I have baptized you with water; he will baptize you with the Holy Spirit."

Reflecting on the Word

Today's Gospel begins with a quote from Isaiah, telling us about a prophet who will come to prepare the way for the Lord. John the Baptist was the prophet sent from God to help people get ready for Jesus' coming by inviting them to repent from their sins and to turn their hearts to the Lord. As we continue our preparations for Christmas, how do we ensure that they aren't just on the outside, but within our hearts as well? Take some time for quiet during this busy season to turn your heart to the Lord.

......ON THE WAY TO MASS

To prepare means to make something ready. What could it mean to "Prepare the way of the Lord"?

ON THE WAY HOME FROM MASS ......

"I have baptized you with water; he will baptize you with the Holy Spirit." What does your baptism have to do with your task of preparing the way of the Lord?

Living the Word

John the Baptist prepared the way for the coming of the Messiah. How can we prepare our hearts and our homes for the coming of Jesus? At this time of year, many families are putting up decorations to prepare for Christmas. Take some time to pray together and bless your Christmas tree or Nativity scene. You can bless your tree using a simple prayer service like the one found here: www.usccb.org/prayers/blessing-christmas-tree.

December 17, 2023

Third Sunday of Advent

Hearing the Word

John 1:6–8, 23–28

In the name of the Father, and of the Son, and of the Holy Spirit.

A man named John was sent from God. He came for testimony, to testify to the light, so that all might believe through him. He was not the light, but came to testify to the light.

[John] said: "I am *the voice of one crying in the desert, 'Make straight the way of the Lord,'* as Isaiah the prophet said." Some Pharisees were also sent. They asked him, "Why then do you baptize if you are not the Christ or Elijah or the Prophet?" John answered them, "I baptize with water; but there is one among you whom you do not recognize, the one who is coming after me, whose sandal strap I am not worthy to untie." This happened in Bethany across the Jordan, where John was baptizing.

Reflecting on the Word

John the Baptist's entire mission is to point others to Jesus. This is our role as parents, yes? We lead our children to Jesus in many ways—by displaying images of Jesus in our home, by praying and saying the holy name of Jesus, and by teaching our children how to make the sign of the cross and the appropriate gestures and responses at Mass. Sharing our faith with our children is a big and important task, and at times, we, like John, may feel unworthy of the task. Yet God has called us to point our children to Jesus! As you seek to do this, invite the Holy Spirit to guide you.

······ ON THE WAY TO MASS

What does it mean to be a witness?

ON THE WAY HOME FROM MASS ······

How does John the Baptist witness to the light who is to come?

Living the Word

In your time together, invite your family members to think of all the ways that Jesus invites us to walk as children of the light. How are we called to speak for the light? How can we testify to the light by the way we live our lives? Light a candle (either a real one or a battery operated one for safety purposes) and place it on the table where your family eats meals together as a reminder of our call bring the light of Christ to those around us.

December 24, 2023

Fourth Sunday of Advent

Hearing the Word
Luke 1:31–38

In the name of the Father, and of the Son, and of the Holy Spirit.

[The angel said, to Mary,] "Behold, you will conceive in your womb and bear a son, and you shall name him Jesus. He will be great and will be called Son of the Most High, and the Lord God will give him the throne of David his father, and he will rule over the house of Jacob forever, and of his kingdom there will be no end." But Mary said to the angel, "How can this be, since I have no relations with a man?" And the angel said to her in reply, "The Holy Spirit will come upon you, and the power of the Most High will overshadow you. Therefore the child to be born will be called holy, the Son of God. And behold, Elizabeth, your relative, has also conceived a son in her old age, and this is the sixth month for her who was called barren; for nothing will be impossible for God." Mary said, "Behold, I am the handmaid of the Lord. May it be done to me according to your word." Then the angel departed from her.

Reflecting on the Word

Today's Gospel invites us to ponder the names of Jesus. First, the angel tells Mary that she will bear a son and that his name will be Jesus. The angel also reveals that this tiny child will also be called Son of the Most High and Son of God. To be given the title "Son of" signifies a very close relationship with God, for Jesus is God made flesh. Finally, the angel also tells us that Jesus comes from a long line of servants of God, descending from both the throne of David and from the house of Jacob, two other mighty names in salvation history. Jesus' identity is so rich, so big, and so mysterious that he cannot be identified by one name or image. Many names are needed for us to understand who he is.

······ ON THE WAY TO MASS

The name Jesus means "one who saves." Listen for how often we refer to Jesus' holy name or to Jesus as Savior during Mass.

ON THE WAY HOME FROM MASS ······

The Holy Spirit was a part of Jesus' birth story. How has the Holy Spirit been with you since the earliest days of your life?

Living the Word

Make a list of all the names of Jesus you can recall. Circle the name you use most often when you talk to Jesus. Underline the name you will use in your prayer this week.

December 25, 2023

Solemnity of the Nativity of the Lord (Mass during the Night)

Hearing the Word

Luke 2:1, 4–7a, 8–14

In the name of the Father, and of the Son, and of the Holy Spirit.

In those days a decree went out from Caesar Augustus that the whole world should be enrolled. And Joseph too went up from Galilee from the town of Nazareth to Judea, to the city of David that is called Bethlehem, because he was of the house and family of David, to be enrolled with Mary, his betrothed, who was with child. While they were there, the time came for her to have her child, and she gave birth to her firstborn son.

Now there were shepherds in that region living in the fields and keeping the night watch over their flock. The angel of the Lord appeared to them and the glory of the Lord shone around them, and they were struck with great fear. The angel said to them, "Do not be afraid; for behold, I proclaim to you good news of great joy that will be for all the people. For today in the city of David a savior has been born for you who is Christ and Lord. And this will be a sign for you: you will find an infant wrapped in swaddling clothes and lying in a manger." And suddenly there was a multitude of the heavenly host with the angel, praising God and saying: / "Glory to God in the highest / and on earth peace to those on whom his favor rests."

Reflecting on the Word

Mary wrapped her baby in swaddling clothes. Newborn babies feel safe and comfortable when they are wrapped in a blanket, nice and snug. Then Mary lays him in a manger, which is a feeding trough for animals. Jesus is so precious, but is placed in a manger where animals feed. This child is born in such humble conditions, and yet will be a gift that brings joy for all people, glory to God, and peace on earth.

......ON THE WAY TO MASS

Today, we will hear about the shepherds who visit the baby Jesus after he was born. Perhaps the shepherds didn't know clearly who Jesus was then, but we do today. What do we know about who Jesus is?

ON THE WAY HOME FROM MASS ......

What did the angel say to the shepherds? "Do not be afraid! A savior has been born! You will find the infant wrapped in swaddling clothes and lying in a manger." Why do you think Jesus came as a helpless baby wrapped in swaddling clothes rather than as a powerful king with an army? What could this mean for us?

Living the Word

What do babies need? Make a list. While we may not be able to purchase items for baby Jesus or for a child in need, we can offer something to Jesus at this moment. Sit quietly at your prayer table or with your Nativity set, tell Jesus what is in your heart. You may say it aloud, quietly in your heart, or write it down as a prayer.

December 31, 2023

Feast of the Holy Family of Jesus, Mary, and Joseph

Hearing the Word

Luke 2:22, 39–40

In the name of the Father, and of the Son, and of the Holy Spirit.

When the days were completed for their purification according to the law of Moses, they took him up to Jerusalem to present him to the Lord.

When they had fulfilled all the prescriptions of the law of the Lord, they returned to Galilee, to their own town of Nazareth. The child grew and became strong, filled with wisdom; and the favor of God was upon him.

Reflecting on the Word

In every community, there are rituals and responsibilities for new parents. Mary and Joseph were obedient to the law of Moses and fulfilled the requirements of the law after Jesus' birth. The child Jesus grew up in this obedience, in this faith. Like Mary and Joseph, we as parents are called to model faith for our children. We do not hear much about the childhood years of Jesus, only that "the child grew and became strong, filled with wisdom; and the favor of God was upon him." How can we make our homes into an environment where our children can grow in faith and find favor with God?

• • • • • • ON THE WAY TO MASS

Baptism is our birth into the family of God; through it, we become members of the Church. Share the story of your children's baptisms with them.

ON THE WAY HOME FROM MASS • • • • • •

Today's Gospel tells us about Jesus, and that the favor of God was upon him. What could this mean, to live in the favor of God?

Living the Word

How do we mark the baptism anniversary of the members of our family? Besides telling the story of the day, display photos (or show a video of the day), the baptismal candle, and the white garment in a special place or prayer table in your home. Ask your parish priest for some holy water and use it at home to bless one another. Finally, write a thank-you letter to godparents and the priest or deacon who baptized each family member.

January 7, 2024

SOLEMNITY OF THE EPIPHANY OF THE LORD

Hearing the Word

Matthew 2:1–5, 7–11

In the name of the Father, and of the Son, and of the Holy Spirit.

When Jesus was born in Bethlehem of Judea, in the days of King Herod, behold, magi from the east arrived in Jerusalem, saying, "Where is the newborn king of the Jews? We saw his star at its rising and have come to do him homage." When King Herod heard this, he was greatly troubled, and all Jerusalem with him. Assembling all the chief priests and the scribes of the people, he inquired of them where the Christ was to be born. They said to him, "In Bethlehem of Judea." Then Herod called the magi secretly and ascertained from them the time of the star's appearance. He sent them to Bethlehem and said, "Go and search diligently for the child. When you have found him, bring me word, that I too may go and do him homage." After their audience with the king they set out. And behold, the star that they had seen at its rising preceded them, until it came and stopped over the place where the child was. They were overjoyed at seeing the star, and on entering the house they saw the child with Mary his mother. They prostrated themselves and did him homage. Then they opened their treasures and offered him gifts of gold, frankincense, and myrrh.

Reflecting on the Word

The Magi are searching for the newborn king. Who is this child? He is a king, who will be offered a tribute of gold. He is recognized as God, which is signified by the gift of incense. Finally, he is also recognized as human with the gift of the myrrh, a perfume used to anoint the dead. Today's Gospel will give us more clues about the identity of this child.

......ON THE WAY TO MASS

The Magi follow the star that leads them to Bethlehem. They saw a large star rising in the sky; why would a small baby have such an amazing star marking his arrival?

ON THE WAY HOME FROM MASS ......

In what ways do the events in today's Gospel tell us more about who Jesus came for? The shepherds lived near Bethlehem, and they were Jewish. What about the Magi?

Living the Word

Even with the star to guide the Magi, they needed more help to find Jesus. Who do we turn to when we need help or advice about what to do, what direction to go? Do we turn to God in prayer? Write a prayer asking God for help for anything that you need help with. Are there other ways we can let God know that we need him?

January 14, 2024

SECOND SUNDAY IN ORDINARY TIME

Hearing the Word

John 1:35–42

In the name of the Father, and of the Son, and of the Holy Spirit.

John was standing with two of his disciples, and as he watched Jesus walk by, he said, "Behold, the Lamb of God." The two disciples heard what he said and followed Jesus. Jesus turned and saw them following him and said to them, "What are you looking for?" They said to him, "Rabbi"—which translated means Teacher—, "where are you staying?" He said to them, "Come, and you will see." So they went and saw where Jesus was staying, and they stayed with him that day. It was about four in the afternoon. Andrew, the brother of Simon Peter, was one of the two who heard John and followed Jesus. He first found his own brother Simon and told him, "We have found the Messiah"—which is translated Christ. Then he brought him to Jesus. Jesus looked at him and said, "You are Simon the son of John; you will be called Cephas"—which is translated Peter.

Reflecting on the Word

As followers of Jesus, we are a part of a community. No one is a disciple of Jesus by themselves. In today's Gospel, Jesus calls two siblings, Andrew and Peter, to be his disciples. Jesus knew how important it is to have family. We all need a community for support and encouragement, and a community to celebrate with and to share our encounters with the Lord. Fortunately, we have a built-in community in our family members! How eager are we to share what we have found with our family members?

•••••• ON THE WAY TO MASS

In today's Gospel Jesus speaks to two disciples. How can we listen for his voice today? How does he speak to us through his Word and the language of signs at Mass? Look for specific gestures at Mass; some gestures are for the priest, other gestures we do as well.

ON THE WAY HOME FROM MASS ••••••

What gestures did you see at Mass? Are there words that accompany any of those gestures? Are there gestures from church that we can do as a family at home?

Living the Word

Our family is the domestic Church, or the Church of the home. We encourage holy habits in the life of our family and perform rituals that help us to follow Jesus. It is important that our children hear the words of the prayers of their parents and vice versa. Invite family members to write a prayer thanking God for your Church of the home and for your parish church. Read your prayers aloud and place them on your prayer table where they can be reread during the week.

January 21, 2024

Third Sunday in Ordinary Time

Hearing the Word

Mark 1:14–20

In the name of the Father, and of the Son, and of the Holy Spirit.

After John had been arrested, Jesus came to Galilee proclaiming the gospel of God: "This is the time of fulfillment. The kingdom of God is at hand. Repent, and believe in the gospel."

As he passed by the Sea of Galilee, he saw Simon and his brother Andrew casting their nets into the sea; they were fishermen. Jesus said to them, "Come after me, and I will make you fishers of men." Then they abandoned their nets and followed him. He walked along a little farther and saw James, the son of Zebedee, and his brother John. They too were in a boat mending their nets. Then he called them. So they left their father Zebedee in the boat along with the hired men and followed him.

Reflecting on the Word

The fishermen abandoned their nets and followed Jesus.
Did they ever question or second-guess that decision?
It appears that they were so sure that they did not hesitate
or offer excuses as to why they could not go. James and
John even left their father in his fishing boat to follow Jesus!
How often do we make excuses for not answering the Lord
when he calls? How can we help our children be still so
that they can hear God calling, and help them to respond
promptly to the working of the Spirit in their lives?

. . . . . . ON THE WAY TO MASS

If Jesus were to ask us today to leave everything behind and follow
him, how might we respond?

ON THE WAY HOME FROM MASS . . . . . .

Simon, Andrew, James, and John all gave up their careers
as fishermen to follow Jesus. What helps us to be able to
follow Jesus?

Living the Word

The fishermen in today's Gospel left everything to follow
Jesus and became "fishers of men." As disciples of Jesus,
they were called to proclaim the Good News of Jesus.
From Mass, we too are sent out to proclaim the Good News.
What story about Jesus would you share? Pick a time this
week to share your stories with one another. Either read the
story from the Bible and tell why that is your favorite or write
it in your own words or draw a scene from the story to share
with your family.

January 28, 2024

Fourth Sunday in Ordinary Time

Hearing the Word

Mark 1:21–28

In the name of the Father, and of the Son, and of the Holy Spirit.

Then they came to Capernaum, and on the sabbath Jesus entered the synagogue and taught. The people were astonished at his teaching, for he taught them as one having authority and not as the scribes. In their synagogue was a man with an unclean spirit; he cried out, "What have you to do with us, Jesus of Nazareth? Have you come to destroy us? I know who you are—the Holy One of God!" Jesus rebuked him and said, "Quiet! Come out of him!" The unclean spirit convulsed him and with a loud cry came out of him. All were amazed and asked one another, "What is this? A new teaching with authority. He commands even the unclean spirits and they obey him." His fame spread everywhere throughout the whole region of Galilee.

Reflecting on the Word

The unclean spirit recognizes Jesus and proclaims his identity, "I know who you are—the Holy One of God!" Yet the people who encounter Jesus in the synagogue are amazed by his teaching and ask one another, "What is this?" How often are we amazed by our encounters with Lord? Do we always recognize his powerful actions in our day-to-day life?

· · · · · · ON THE WAY TO MASS

What does it mean to be holy? How are each of us made holy? Our home is a holy place. How is that made visible?

ON THE WAY HOME FROM MASS · · · · · ·

Why do you think the people listened to Jesus when he talked? Why do you listen to Jesus?

Living the Word

In our creed, we profess that we are one, holy, catholic, and apostolic Church. The word *holy* means to be set apart for a special purpose by and for God. Discuss as a family who you know who has been set apart for God's work. (Hint: It's all of us!) Invite each family member to consider how God is calling him or her to holiness this week.

February 4, 2024

Fifth Sunday in Ordinary Time

Hearing the Word

Mark 1:29–39

In the name of the Father, and of the Son, and of the Holy Spirit.

On leaving the synagogue Jesus entered the house of Simon and Andrew with James and John. Simon's mother-in-law lay sick with a fever. They immediately told him about her. He approached, grasped her hand, and helped her up. Then the fever left her and she waited on them.

When it was evening, after sunset, they brought to him all who were ill or possessed by demons. The whole town was gathered at the door. He cured many who were sick with various diseases, and he drove out many demons, not permitting them to speak because they knew him.

Rising very early before dawn, he left and went off to a deserted place, where he prayed. Simon and those who were with him pursued him and on finding him said, "Everyone is looking for you." He told them, "Let us go on to the nearby villages that I may preach there also. For this purpose have I come." So he went into their synagogues, preaching and driving out demons throughout the whole of Galilee.

Reflecting on the Word

Amid all the busyness we see in today's Gospel, we see that Jesus still takes the time to pray. As parents, as for Jesus, it can feel like people are always coming to us or needing something from us. Jesus shows us that it is particularly in those times that we need to make time for prayer. We need time with the Lord to receive the strength we need to continue the important work of caring for others around us. How can you carve out some time in your day to get away from the busyness of everyday life and spent time in quiet?

...... ON THE WAY TO MASS

How can we make time for prayer in our life together as a family, especially when we are busy?

ON THE WAY HOME FROM MASS ......

When Jesus healed Peter's mother-in-law, she got up and waited on them. What is your response when someone has shown you compassion?

Living the Word

Jesus shows compassion by healing Peter's mother-in-law. We too, are called to show compassion to those who are sick. Create a get-well card for someone who is sick or a thinking-of-you note for an elderly person in your neighborhood. If you do not know of anyone to send them to, offer the correspondence to your parish priest or other pastoral care minister to take on their visits to the sick and homebound.

February 11, 2024

Sixth Sunday in Ordinary Time

Hearing the Word

Mark 1:40–45

In the name of the Father, and of the Son, and of the Holy Spirit.

A leper came to Jesus and kneeling down begged him and said, "If you wish, you can make me clean." Moved with pity, he stretched out his hand, touched him, and said to him, "I do will it. Be made clean." The leprosy left him immediately, and he was made clean. Then, warning him sternly, he dismissed him at once.

Then He said to him, "See that you tell no one anything, but go, show yourself to the priest and offer for your cleansing what Moses prescribed; that will be proof for them."

The man went away and began to publicize the whole matter. He spread the report abroad so that it was impossible for Jesus to enter a town openly. He remained outside in deserted places, and people kept coming to him from everywhere.

Reflecting on the Word

Jesus meets a leper, who begs to be made clean. To be clean meant that the leper could rejoin the community, rather than live as an outcast. Jesus was able to see this man with the eyes of compassion and to offer him a way out of his life of suffering. When we experience pain, misery, and anguish, we realize how much we need one another and God. How can we share God's love and closeness with those who feel cut off from the support of the community?

......ON THE WAY TO MASS

Have you ever felt left out, excluded, or cut off from others? How would it feel to be included again?

ON THE WAY HOME FROM MASS ......

During the week, we may get busy with schoolwork, household chores, or other things that fill our days. In these times, how can we remember to turn to Jesus for help when we are in need?

Living the Word

Our elderly or shut-in friends may feel that they have been forgotten and excluded from society. How can your family reach out and include an elderly neighbor, a retired priest or sister, or help a homebound parishioner feel more connected and included? Write a letter, make a phone call, draw a picture, bake a treat, and let them know how much they mean to your family. Be sure to share stories, memories, and smiles.

February 18, 2024

First Sunday of Lent

Hearing the Word
Mark 1:12–15

In the name of the Father, and of the Son, and of the Holy Spirit.

The Spirit drove Jesus out into the desert, and he remained in the desert for forty days, tempted by Satan. He was among wild beasts, and the angels ministered to him.

After John had been arrested, Jesus came to Galilee proclaiming the gospel of God: "This is the time of fulfillment. The kingdom of God is at hand. Repent, and believe in the gospel."

Reflecting on the Word

In today's Gospel, Jesus goes into the desert for forty days to pray and is tempted by Satan. He is among wild beasts, and the angels come to minister to him. Jesus needs this time of preparation before he begins his public ministry. What about our own preparation? Is it easy to prepare when illness, suffering, and temptation surround us? How do you prepare yourself and your family for those times that seem to be especially challenging?

......ON THE WAY TO MASS

Sometimes we make good choices, and sometimes we are tempted to go against God's plan. Reflect on the last time you made a good choice that yielded harmony, unity, and peace.

ON THE WAY HOME FROM MASS ......

Jesus went to the desert to pray. What does that tell us about how we can prepare ourselves to make good choices? Praying and reading God's Word, the Bible, will help us stay close to him.

Living the Word

For your prayer table at home, find a piece of purple cloth, a purple scarf or pillowcase, or even some purple construction paper to place on the table. Changing the color of the cloth is a way for the children to focus on and to honor the same change that they will observe in the parish church. As a family, decide what other items will adorn your prayer table during Lent: a Bible, a candle, a crucifix? Is there a word or phrase from today's Gospel that you would like to include on your prayer table?

February 25, 2024

Second Sunday of Lent

Hearing the Word
Mark 9:2–10

In the name of the Father, and of the Son, and of the Holy Spirit.

Jesus took Peter, James, and John and led them up a high mountain apart by themselves. And he was transfigured before them, and his clothes became dazzling white, such as no fuller on earth could bleach them. Then Elijah appeared to them along with Moses, and they were conversing with Jesus. Then Peter said to Jesus in reply, "Rabbi, it is good that we are here! Let us make three tents: one for you, one for Moses, and one for Elijah." He hardly knew what to say, they were so terrified. Then a cloud came, casting a shadow over them; from the cloud came a voice, "This is my beloved Son. Listen to him." Suddenly, looking around, they no longer saw anyone but Jesus alone with them.

As they were coming down from the mountain, he charged them not to relate what they had seen to anyone, except when the Son of Man had risen from the dead. So they kept the matter to themselves, questioning what rising from the dead meant.

Reflecting on the Word

In today's Gospel, Peter, James, and John witness the Transfiguration of Jesus on Mount Tabor. Moses and Elijah appear on either side of Jesus, showing us that the Law and the Prophets direct people to Jesus, in whom the full glory of God is manifest. The three disciples did not experience this as individuals, but as a group, in community. The family is a community in which we can experience the glory of God. How have we experienced this in the sacraments, in the beauty and wonder of nature, or in our life as the domestic Church?

...... ON THE WAY TO MASS

We pray a prayer at Mass called the Gloria. Be sure to listen to the words: "We praise you, / we bless you, / we adore you, / we glorify you."

ON THE WAY HOME FROM MASS ......

What do you imagine the glory of the Lord looks like? How can we give God glory? What would that look like?

Living the Word

Make a prayer card for your family prayer table, or as a centerpiece on your dining room table, that reads GLORY TO GOD. Pray the Gloria prayer from Mass or the Glory Be prayer each night this week. Discuss when and where you have experienced the glory of God.

Third Sunday of Lent

Hearing the Word

John 2:13–22

In the name of the Father, and of the Son, and of the Holy Spirit.

Since the Passover of the Jews was near, Jesus went up to Jerusalem. He found in the temple area those who sold oxen, sheep, and doves, as well as the money changers seated there. He made a whip out of cords and drove them all out of the temple area, with the sheep and oxen, and spilled the coins of the money changers and overturned their tables, and to those who sold doves he said, "Take these out of here, and stop making my Father's house a marketplace." His disciples recalled the words of Scripture, / *Zeal for your house will consume me. /* At this the Jews answered and said to him, "What sign can you show us for doing this?" Jesus answered and said to them, "Destroy this temple and in three days I will raise it up." The Jews said, "This temple has been under construction for forty-six years, and you will raise it up in three days?" But he was speaking about the temple of his body. Therefore, when he was raised from the dead, his disciples remembered that he had said this, and they came to believe the Scripture and the word Jesus had spoken.

Reflecting on the Word

Jesus' cleansing of the temple is a rather challenging Scripture passage because it describes Jesus' anger. Is he angry at the money changers? Is he frustrated about how the temple is being used by those selling animals and exchanging money? Or is it the way this system of worshipping God has seemed to put a myriad of rules and regulations between the individual and God? As parents, we too have moments when we get angry or frustrated. In these moments, we can lean on Jesus, who, being fully human, knows what we are going through.

· · · · · ·ON THE WAY TO MASS

Our church is a sacred, holy place. It is a place where God dwells in a most particular way. He is present in the gathered assembly, when the Word is proclaimed, and when the Bread is broken. How can we help make this environment even more holy today?

ON THE WAY HOME FROM MASS · · · · · ·

Today, we heard how Jesus got angry in the temple. He later told the people, "Destroy this temple, and in three days I will raise it up." We know that anything that has been broken, Jesus can restore. What in your life would you like Jesus to heal or restore?

Living the Word

Over the next few days, talk together about one act that might bring Jesus' healing love to the family, to the neighborhood, to the world. Make a list of ideas and choose one that has meaning for the whole family.

March 10, 2024

Fourth Sunday of Lent

Hearing the Word
John 3:14–21

In the name of the Father, and of the Son, and of the Holy Spirit.

Jesus said to Nicodemus: "Just as Moses lifted up the serpent in the desert, so must the Son of Man be lifted up, so that everyone who believes in him may have eternal life."

For God so loved the world that he gave his only Son, so that everyone who believes in him might not perish but might have eternal life. For God did not send his Son into the world to condemn the world, but that the world might be saved through him. Whoever believes in him will not be condemned, but whoever does not believe has already been condemned, because he has not believed in the name of the only Son of God. And this is the verdict, that the light came into the world, but people preferred darkness to light, because their works were evil. For everyone who does wicked things hates the light and does not come toward the light, so that his works might not be exposed. But whoever lives the truth comes to the light, so that his works may be clearly seen as done in God.

Reflecting on the Word

Jesus tells Nicodemus that he is the light that has come into the world. Some days it seems like the darkness is going to overtake the light, but we know that the light is stronger than darkness, that his love is stronger than hate, and that his risen life is stronger than death. Children are often afraid of the dark and know that great comfort is found in the light. God made us to live in and walk in the light.

......ON THE WAY TO MASS

How does it feel to be alone in a dark room? How does it feel when the light is turned on? Jesus said, "I am the light." Imagine his light all over the world. At Mass, servers often carry lit candles to the ambo and hold them while the Gospel is read. The candles remind us that Jesus is the light of the world. When the Scriptures are proclaimed, Jesus' light is present to us.

ON THE WAY HOME FROM MASS ......

Jesus told Nicodemus that the people need to come toward the light. What can that mean for us to come toward the light?

Living the Word

Count the lights you have in your home: lamps, lightbulbs, flashlights, nightlights, porch light, candles, lanterns, and so on. What would your home be like if you could not use the gift of light? Just as we need light in our homes, we need the light of Christ to enlighten us. Pray together that the light of Christ would shine more brightly in your home and in your life this week.

March 17, 2024

Fifth Sunday of Lent

Hearing the Word

John 12:23–30

In the name of the Father, and of the Son, and of the Holy Spirit.

Jesus answered them, "The hour has come for the Son of Man to be glorified. Amen, amen, I say to you, unless a grain of wheat falls to the ground and dies, it remains just a grain of wheat; but if it dies, it produces much fruit. Whoever loves his life loses it, and whoever hates his life in this world will preserve it for eternal life. Whoever serves me must follow me, and where I am, there also will my servant be. The Father will honor whoever serves me.

"I am troubled now. Yet what should I say? 'Father, save me from this hour'? But it was for this purpose that I came to this hour. Father, glorify your name." Then a voice came from heaven, "I have glorified it and will glorify it again." The crowd there heard it and said it was thunder; but others said, "An angel has spoken to him." Jesus answered and said, "This voice did not come for my sake but for yours. Now is the time of judgment on this world; now the ruler of this world will be driven out. And when I am lifted up from the earth, I will draw everyone to myself." He said this indicating the kind of death he would die.

Reflecting on the Word

Jesus cared for his friends and prepared them for his death. He knew that they would be sad, and that they would have a hard time understanding what was about to happen to him. To help them, Jesus spoke about a grain of wheat that falls to the ground and dies. Unless the seed dies, it could only be one small seed. But if it dies, something amazing and wonderful happens. From one little seed comes tremendous growth. Jesus' words give us reassurance that death is not the end, and that God has the power to bring great good even out of moments of hurt and sorrow.

......ON THE WAY TO MASS

At Mass today we will hear Jesus tells us about a seed. What happens to a seed when it goes into the soil? What does a seed need to grow?

ON THE WAY HOME FROM MASS ......

Why do you think Jesus tells us the seed must die before it can grow? The seed has died when it is under the soil, and a little plant comes to birth. If the seed has died, is it finished?

Living the Word

When the seed goes into the soil, we do not see anything; the seed is covered. What happens to the seed, happens in the darkness, but there is a great force within the seed. Plant some seeds in a small pot and observe them each day. Make a log of what you notice happening as time passes. How is God at work in us, bringing new life even out of imperfect or difficult circumstances?

March 24, 2024

Palm Sunday of the Passion of the Lord

Hearing the Word
Mark 11:1–2, 7–10

In the name of the Father, and of the Son, and of the Holy Spirit.

When Jesus and his disciples drew near to Jerusalem, to Bethpage and Bethany at the Mount of Olives, he sent two of his disciples and said to them, "Go into the village opposite you, and immediately on entering it, you will find a colt tethered on which no one has ever sat. Untie it and bring it here." So they brought the colt to Jesus and put their cloaks over it. And he sat on it. Many people spread their cloaks on the road, and others spread leafy branches that they had cut from the fields. Those preceding him as well as those following kept crying out: / "Hosanna! / Blessed is he who comes in the name of the Lord! / Blessed is the kingdom of our father David that is to come! / Hosanna in the highest!"

Reflecting on the Word

The people praise Jesus today, and we will echo the words the people shout as Jesus enters the city of Jerusalem: "Hosanna!" Hosanna is a word found in the Book of Psalms and is a cry for help. It means, "Save us, we pray!" We have all experienced challenges in parenthood, whether at the birth of a child, during toddlerhood, or school age. We sometimes feel alone in our struggles, not realizing that God is present in all those moments of difficulty, ready to listen to our cries, and respond to our prayers.

......ON THE WAY TO MASS

In today's Gospel, the people lay their cloaks on the road in front of Jesus as he enters Jerusalem. Others lay palm branches on the ground. This is one way that the people honor Jesus. How will we honor him at Mass today?

ON THE WAY HOME FROM MASS ......

As he entered Jerusalem, the people treated Jesus like a king. What did they say? Where have we heard those words before? How do these words give honor and praise to Jesus? How can I praise him this week?

Living the Word

Write a prayer of praise to Jesus or decorate a prayer card with the word Hosanna. Imagine Jesus is coming to your hometown today, riding on a colt. Discuss how your family would greet Jesus.

March 31, 2024

Easter Sunday of the Resurrection of the Lord

Hearing the Word

Mark 16:1–7

In the name of the Father, and of the Son, and of the Holy Spirit.

When the sabbath was over, Mary Magdalene, Mary, the mother of James, and Salome bought spices so that they might go and anoint him. Very early when the sun had risen, on the first day of the week, they came to the tomb. They were saying to one another, "Who will roll back the stone for us from the entrance to the tomb?" When they looked up, they saw that the stone had been rolled back; it was very large. On entering the tomb they saw a young man sitting on the right side, clothed in a white robe, and they were utterly amazed. He said to them, "Do not be amazed! You seek Jesus of Nazareth, the crucified. He has been raised; he is not here. Behold the place where they laid him. But go and tell his disciples and Peter, 'He is going before you to Galilee; there you will see him, as he told you.'"

Reflecting on the Word

As parents, we are concerned with the details of daily life (who will roll back the stone for us), and we often find what we are worried and concerned about had already been taken care of (the stone was already moved). This Easter, may we, like the women at the tomb, encounter the surprise, the amazement, the joy of God's plan being fulfilled in the resurrection of his Son. Even in our worry, doubt, or confusion, let us be restored and find our hope in the risen Christ.

......ON THE WAY TO MASS

In today's Gospel, the women at the tomb were utterly amazed. When was the last time you were truly amazed by something?

ON THE WAY HOME FROM MASS ......

The women at the tomb were changed by the events of that first Easter morning. How do the events of that day make a difference in my life today?

Living the Word

Jesus rose from the dead two thousand years ago. Think about all the people in your life whose lives have been transformed by the risen Christ. Make a timeline and list all the people in your family, going back as many generations as possible. Widen your list to include people in your neighborhood, or people in your Church (including the saints) who were transformed by Jesus' resurrection. God has a plan for all of creation to enjoy fullness of life with him. Leave some space on the front of your timeline to write about how you are working with God to bring about his plan.

April 7, 2024

Second Sunday of Easter / Sunday of Divine Mercy

Hearing the Word

John 20:19–23

In the name of the Father, and of the Son, and of the Holy Spirit.

On the evening of that first day of the week, when the doors were locked, where the disciples were, for fear of the Jews, Jesus came and stood in their midst and said to them, "Peace be with you." When he had said this, he showed them his hands and his side. The disciples rejoiced when they saw the Lord. Jesus said to them again, "Peace be with you. As the Father has sent me, so I send you." And when he had said this, he breathed on them and said to them, "Receive the Holy Spirit. Whose sins you forgive are forgiven them, and whose sins you retain are retained."

Reflecting on the Word

When there are disagreements among family members, we are encouraged to "make peace" and shake hands or embrace the other. Sometimes we are not ready to embrace one another in an act of peace. How are we able to practice sharing peace with one another? In today's Gospel, Jesus stood in their midst and said to them, "Peace be with you." How do we allow Jesus to enter those moments of forgiveness and peace in our home? Is it easier to make peace when we are aware of his presence?

......ON THE WAY TO MASS

What do you think of when you hear the word *peace*? What does it mean when we greet one another with the words "May the peace of Christ be with you?" What are we wishing for the other person?

ON THE WAY HOME FROM MASS ......

Why do you think Jesus' first word to his disciples after the resurrection was peace?

Living the Word

As a family, look for instances of peace, harmony, or contentment in your week. Have your children write about them or draw an image of those moments, and then to share those moments with the family.

April 14, 2024

Third Sunday of Easter

Hearing the Word

Luke 24:36–40, 44–48

In the name of the Father, and of the Son, and of the Holy Spirit.

[Jesus] stood in their midst and said to them, "Peace be with you." But they were startled and terrified and thought that they were seeing a ghost. Then he said to them, "Why are you troubled? And why do questions arise in your hearts? Look at my hands and my feet, that it is I myself. Touch me and see, because a ghost does not have flesh and bones as you can see I have." And as he said this, he showed them his hands and his feet.

He said to them, "These are my words that I spoke to you while I was still with you, that everything written about me in the law of Moses and in the prophets and psalms must be fulfilled." Then he opened their minds to understand the Scriptures. And he said to them, "Thus it is written that the Christ would suffer and rise from the dead on the third day and that repentance, for the forgiveness of sins, would be preached in his name to all the nations, beginning from Jerusalem. You are witnesses of these things."

Reflecting on the Word

When one of our children has a frightening dream, we want to hold them and soothe them. When we have moments of fear, we too, need to be consoled by the one who can give us the sense that all will be well. It is easy to trust him when all is well in our lives, but when we are "startled and terrified" by life, we also need to turn to him. It is in those moments that we must witness to the world of his faithful love, and how we trust in his comfort and care.

•••••• ON THE WAY TO MASS

What do you think it would have been like for the disciples to see Jesus risen? Why do you think they were afraid at first?

ON THE WAY HOME FROM MASS ••••••

Jesus told the disciples that they were to be witnesses to the Good News. Is it only the disciples who are witnesses to the Gospel? How are we called to be a witness to the risen Christ?

Living the Word

As you gather for your evening meal, think about how you have witnessed the love of the risen Christ today. Where did you see his love present? Did you happen to get a glimpse of it at home? In your neighborhood? At church? Read about it in a book or online? Or did you see it in nature, maybe in your own yard or in the park? Let everyone share their own witness story. If you did not see one today, be mindful of looking for glimpses this week.

April 21, 2024

Fourth Sunday of Easter

Hearing the Word

John 10:11–18

In the name of the Father, and of the Son, and of the Holy Spirit.

Jesus said: "I am the good shepherd. A good shepherd lays down his life for the sheep. A hired man, who is not a shepherd and whose sheep are not his own, sees a wolf coming and leaves the sheep and runs away, and the wolf catches and scatters them. This is because he works for pay and has no concern for the sheep. I am the good shepherd, and I know mine and mine know me, just as the Father knows me and I know the Father; and I will lay down my life for the sheep. I have other sheep that do not belong to this fold. These also I must lead, and they will hear my voice, and there will be one flock, one shepherd. This is why the Father loves me, because I lay down my life in order to take it up again. No one takes it from me, but I lay it down on my own. I have power to lay it down, and power to take it up again. This command I have received from my Father."

Reflecting on the Word

The Good Shepherd loves and cares for the sheep. He knows each of the sheep by name. He calls them and they follow his voice. How do we recognize the voice of the Good Shepherd amid the noise and competing voices in the world? We know the voice of the Good Shepherd because we have heard his Word so often. It is in listening to him that we know about his great love for us. The great self-sacrificing love that the Good Shepherd has for the sheep reminds us of the love that the parent has for the child.

......ON THE WAY TO MASS

In today's Gospel, Jesus tells us that he is the Good Shepherd. What does a shepherd do? What do sheep need?

ON THE WAY HOME FROM MASS ......

The Good Shepherd calls us by name. We listen to his voice so that we can follow him. How far does his voice reach?

Living the Word

We listen to the Good Shepherd's voice and follow him. One of the ways we listen to his voice is by reading his Word. Spend time this week reading about the love and care of the Shepherd in Psalm 23. This psalm tells us that the Shepherd gives us everything we need, including comfort and courage when we are afraid. Have each member of your family illustrate a line from this psalm. Collect all the images to make a Psalm 23 booklet.

April 28, 2024

Fifth Sunday of Easter

Hearing the Word

John 15:1–8

In the name of the Father, and of the Son, and of the Holy Spirit.

Jesus said to his disciples: "I am the true vine, and my Father is the vine grower. He takes away every branch in me that does not bear fruit, and every one that does he prunes so that it bears more fruit. You are already pruned because of the word that I spoke to you. Remain in me, as I remain in you. Just as a branch cannot bear fruit on its own unless it remains on the vine, so neither can you unless you remain in me. I am the vine, you are the branches. Whoever remains in me and I in him will bear much fruit, because without me you can do nothing. Anyone who does not remain in me will be thrown out like a branch and wither; people will gather them and throw them into a fire and they will be burned. If you remain in me and my words remain in you, ask for whatever you want and it will be done for you. By this is my Father glorified, that you bear much fruit and become my disciples."

Reflecting on the Word

Our children desire a close and loving relationship with us.
They do not desire things, but rather our time with them.
They want us to put away technology and focus on connecting
with them. Their greatest desire is to be in relationship. Jesus
invites us to remain in him, to be in a close and loving relationship with him. Jesus asks us to stay close to him. Consider
how our children's desire for closeness with us can serve as
a reminder of the closeness the Lord calls us to with himself.

...... ON THE WAY TO MASS

What does it mean to remain? We will hear this word often
at Mass today. Listen for this word and think about why Jesus
says it so often.

ON THE WAY HOME FROM MASS ......

We have already listened to his voice and come to him.
Now he asks us to remain, to stay with him. How do we do so?

Living the Word

We know that a grapevine produces grapes, from which
comes grape jelly, grape juice, and even wine. Jesus is the
true vine and we are the branches. If the life and love of the
Holy Spirit are inside us, what will be visible on the outside?
Will others be able to see by what we do and by what we say
that the life and love of God is inside us? Enjoy a grape-inspired
snack and talk about how you see each family member
bearing fruit.

May 5, 2024

Sixth Sunday of Easter

Hearing the Word

John 15:9–17

In the name of the Father, and of the Son, and of the Holy Spirit.

Jesus said to his disciples: "As the Father loves me, so I also love you. Remain in my love. If you keep my commandments, you will remain in my love, just as I have kept my Father's commandments and remain in his love.

"I have told you this so that my joy may be in you and your joy might be complete. This is my commandment: love one another as I love you. No one has greater love than this, to lay down one's life for one's friends. You are my friends if you do what I command you. I no longer call you slaves, because a slave does not know what his master is doing. I have called you friends, because I have told you everything I have heard from my Father. It was not you who chose me, but I who chose you and appointed you to go and bear fruit that will remain, so that whatever you ask the Father in my name he may give you. This I command you: love one another."

Reflecting on the Word

Jesus wants a close and loving relationship with us, and he promises a full life of complete joy. He shows us that to find joy we must love one another. Jesus wants to be a model for our loving; we can look at how he loves and see how we ought to love others in return. Of course, sometimes this is difficult for us to do, even for us to love those in our own family. But the Gospel tells us that we did not choose Jesus; he chose us. In choosing us, he gives us the strength to love one another, even when it is difficult.

ON THE WAY TO MASS

What do you love about your friends? What do you like to do with your friends? In today's Gospel, Jesus calls us friends. How would others know that Jesus is my friend? How do my words, my actions, and what is in my heart show Jesus that he is my friend?

ON THE WAY HOME FROM MASS • • • • • •

Jesus said, "I have told you this so that my joy may be in you and that your joy may be complete." How would you describe complete joy?

Living the Word

Jesus invites us to love one another. What does that look like in your family, your neighborhood, your school, or your work environment? Make a list of (1) how you have loved others this week, and (2) how others have shown you love this week. Which list is longer? How might this inspire or challenge you as you strive to follow the command to love others this week?

May 9/12, 2024

SOLEMNITY OF THE ASCENSION OF THE LORD

Hearing the Word
Mark 16:15–20

In the name of the Father, and of the Son, and of the Holy Spirit.

Jesus said to his disciples: "Go into the whole world and proclaim the gospel to every creature. Whoever believes and is baptized will be saved; whoever does not believe will be condemned. These signs will accompany those who believe: in my name they will drive out demons, they will speak new languages. They will pick up serpents with their hands, and if they drink any deadly thing, it will not harm them. They will lay hands on the sick, and they will recover."

So then the Lord Jesus, after he spoke to them, was taken up into heaven and took his seat at the right hand of God. But they went forth and preached everywhere, while the Lord worked with them and confirmed the word through accompanying signs.

Reflecting on the Word

Today, we hear Jesus instructing the disciples to go out into the world and proclaim the Good News to every creature. As parents, we are called to proclaim the Good News within our families. We do so when we pray and read the Bible together, and when we share about the love of Jesus. While they may not be moments of miraculous healing, we encounter God's healing when we dry a child's tears or care for a child's skinned knee. The Good News is proclaimed and lived in the life of our family.

......ON THE WAY TO MASS

Jesus' time on earth draws to a close with his ascension, but his mission continues. How does the Church carry on the mission of Jesus in the world today? How do we participate in that work?

ON THE WAY HOME FROM MASS ......

Jesus speaks of miraculous signs that accompany those who believe in him. What signs in our lives show others that we believe in Jesus?

Living the Word

Jesus told the disciples to go into to the whole world and proclaim the Gospel to every creature. How does your family proclaim the Gospel to one another? to those outside your home? Jesus helped the disciples after he ascended to heaven. Discuss how Jesus continues to help us as we follow him.

May 12, 2024

Seventh Sunday of Easter

Hearing the Word

John 17:11b–19

In the name of the Father, and of the Son, and of the Holy Spirit.

Lifting up his eyes to heaven, Jesus prayed, saying: "Holy Father, keep them in your name that you have given me, so that they may be one just as we are one. When I was with them I protected them in your name that you gave me, and I guarded them, and none of them was lost except the son of destruction, in order that the Scripture might be fulfilled. But now I am coming to you. I speak this in the world so that they may share my joy completely. I gave them your word, and the world hated them, because they do not belong to the world any more than I belong to the world. I do not ask that you take them out of the world but that you keep them from the evil one. They do not belong to the world any more than I belong to the world. Consecrate them in the truth. Your word is truth. As you sent me into the world, so I sent them into the world. And I consecrate myself for them, so that they also may be consecrated in truth."

Reflecting on the Word

How often has someone asked you to pray for them? How often have you asked a friend to remember your intentions in their prayers? It is a great comfort to know that others are lifting us up in prayer, and we feel connected to others when we pray for them. Today, we hear a beautiful prayer of Jesus in which he prays for all his disciples—including us. Jesus prays that his disciples receive his joy, his protection from the evil one, and he also prays for them to be consecrated in truth. How does it feel to know that Jesus offered these prayers not only for the disciples of long ago, but for each of us today?

......ON THE WAY TO MASS

Jesus loves his friends and prays for them. Who can you pray for today? Is there a friend or family member who needs your prayers?

ON THE WAY HOME FROM MASS ......

How does your prayer life show that you are among Jesus' good friends?

Living the Word

Make a family prayer jar (or a family prayer bowl). Include some strips of paper so that family members may write down their daily prayer intentions. Schedule a time for prayer each day and plan where the family can sit quietly and write (or draw) their prayer requests. You may want to look in the newspaper to see who in the community or world needs prayer. Each night (or at the end of the week), read the intentions aloud. Add any spontaneous prayers and songs of praise and thanksgiving to God.

May 19, 2024

Pentecost Sunday

Hearing the Word
John 15:26–27; 16:12–15

In the name of the Father, and of the Son, and of the Holy Spirit.

Jesus said to his disciples: "When the Advocate comes whom I will send you from the Father, the Spirit of truth that proceeds from the Father, he will testify to me. And you also testify, because you have been with me from the beginning.

"I have much more to tell you, but you cannot bear it now. But when he comes, the Spirit of truth, he will guide you to all truth. He will not speak on his own, but he will speak what he hears, and will declare to you the things that are coming. He will glorify me, because he will take from what is mine and declare it to you. Everything that the Father has is mine; for this reason I told you that he will take from what is mine and declare it to you."

Reflecting on the Word

Jesus promises to send the Holy Spirit, the Advocate, who will be a guide for us and bear witness to Jesus and remind us of all that he has shared with us. Do we easily recognize the presence of the Holy Spirit in our lives? How do we lean into the guidance of the Holy Spirit when we need assistance? As parents, we are called to care for and protect our children, both physically and spiritually. Think of all the ways you guide your children throughout all the changing years of your family's life. Thank the Holy Spirit for helping your family to make decisions out of a spirit of love.

•••••• ON THE WAY TO MASS

Today at Mass we will see red decorating the altar and worn by the priest. Red is the color of the Holy Spirit. It is also the color of great love. What does the Holy Spirit have to do with love?

ON THE WAY HOME FROM MASS ••••••

Do you know of anyone who is filled with the Holy Spirit? How do you know they are full of the Holy Spirit?

Living the Word

To help the family focus on the Holy Spirit, make a prayer card with the words "Come, Holy Spirit." Write a family litany to the Holy Spirit. Each line of the prayer could focus on how the family might recognize the presence of the Holy Spirit in the world, or how we (or the world) need the guidance of the Holy Spirit. Pray your litany and after each line, say, "Come, Holy Spirit."

May 26, 2024

Solemnity of the Most Holy Trinity

Hearing the Word

Matthew 28:16–20

In the name of the Father, and of the Son, and of the Holy Spirit.

The eleven disciples went to Galilee, to the mountain to which Jesus had ordered them. When they all saw him, they worshiped, but they doubted. Then Jesus approached and said to them, "All power in heaven and on earth has been given to me. Go, therefore, and make disciples of all nations, baptizing them in the name of the Father, and of the Son, and of the Holy Spirit, teaching them to observe all that I have commanded you. And behold, I am with you always, until the end of the age."

Reflecting on the Word

Jesus tells his disciples to baptize in the name of the Father, and of the Son, and of the Holy Spirit. Plunged into the waters of baptism, we pass through the death of Jesus and rise to new life in God, the Holy Trinity, whom we celebrate this day. Ask your parish priest for a bottle of holy water (if you don't have one already), which you can keep in your home and use to remind you of the cross and the water in which you were baptized.

• • • • • • ON THE WAY TO MASS

Did you know there is a special gesture that we can make when we want to remember that we belong to God, who is Father, Son, and Holy Spirit? It is a gesture that we see at Mass, and we can also make this gesture at home, or any time we want to remember how close Jesus is to us. It's the sign of the cross! How many times we will see this gesture at Mass today?

ON THE WAY HOME FROM MASS • • • • • •

The sign of the cross is the holiest of signs. We can sign ourselves when we are tempted, so that we can be strengthened. We can sign ourselves when we fear harm, so we may be protected. At what other times do we sign ourselves with this sacred sign?

Living the Word

The Church Fathers wrote about the sign of the cross and likened it to a seal by which the Shepherd can recognize his sheep. At baptism, we are signed with the cross. Write out the words of the prayer and be intentional with how you make the gesture, making sure not to rush, but do so slowly and reverently, touching forehead, chest, and shoulder to shoulder.

June 2, 2024

Solemnity of the Most Holy Body and Blood of Christ

Hearing the Word

Mark 14:12–16, 22–26

In the name of the Father, and of the Son, and of the Holy Spirit.

On the first day of the Feast of Unleavened Bread, when they sacrificed the Passover lamb, Jesus' disciples said to him, "Where do you want us to go and prepare for you to eat the Passover?" He sent two of his disciples and said to them, "Go into the city and a man will meet you, carrying a jar of water. Follow him. Wherever he enters, say to the master of the house, 'The Teacher says, "Where is my guest room where I may eat the Passover with my disciples?"'" Then he will show you a large upper room furnished and ready. Make the preparations for us there." The disciples then went off, entered the city, and found it just as he had told them; and they prepared the Passover.

While they were eating, he took bread, said the blessing, broke it, gave it to them, and said, "Take it; this is my body." Then he took a cup, gave thanks, and gave it to them, and they all drank from it. He said to them, "This is my blood of the covenant, which will be shed for many. Amen, I say to you, I shall not drink again the fruit of the vine until the day when I drink it new in the kingdom of God." Then, after singing a hymn, they went out to the Mount of Olives.

Reflecting on the Word

Today, we will hear words of great love said over the bread, "Take and eat, this is my body," and over the wine, "This is my blood of the covenant, which will be shed for many." Jesus proclaimed these words at the Last Supper, and the priest prays them at every Mass. Think about all the people in the long history of the Church who have participated in the Mass. Think about your parents, grandparents, and ancestors in faith, who have heard these words of love. Now you continue this tradition, so that the next generation may participate more fully in the life of the Church.

......ON THE WAY TO MASS

Today, we celebrate the Solemnity of the Most Holy Body and Blood of Christ. Let us listen for the words "Take and eat, this is my body," and "This is my blood of the covenant" that Jesus proclaimed at the Last Supper and that the priest prays at every Mass.

ON THE WAY HOME FROM MASS ......

What do you think about the fact that the Church still prays the same words that Jesus said at the Last Supper over two thousand years ago? Isn't it amazing that we are still hearing these words?

Living the Word

The word *Eucharist* means thanksgiving. What can we thank God for today? How can we express our thankfulness when we go to Mass? Make a family "thanks be to God" list. Write down all the things you are thankful for, and next to each entry, write how you can show God that you give him thanks.

June 9, 2024

Tenth Sunday in Ordinary Time

Hearing the Word

Mark 3:20–30

In the name of the Father, and of the Son, and of the Holy Spirit.

Jesus came home with his disciples. Again the crowd gathered, making it impossible for them even to eat. When his relatives heard of this they set out to seize him, for they said, "He is out of his mind." The scribes who had come from Jerusalem said, "He is possessed by Beelzebul," and "By the prince of demons he drives out demons."

Summoning them, he began to speak to them in parables, "How can Satan drive out Satan? If a kingdom is divided against itself, that kingdom cannot stand. And if a house is divided against itself, that house will not be able to stand. And if Satan has risen up against himself and is divided, he cannot stand; that is the end of him. But no one can enter a strong man's house to plunder his property unless he first ties up the strong man. Then he can plunder the house. Amen, I say to you, all sins and all blasphemies that people utter will be forgiven them. But whoever blasphemes against the Holy Spirit will never have forgiveness, but is guilty of an everlasting sin." For they had said, "He has an unclean spirit."

Reflecting on the Word

Jesus' family could not understand his ministry and set out to seize him saying, "He is out of his mind." Maybe we have had similar thoughts about our own family members, or someone in your own family may have judged you without fully understanding. We are not always able to agree with our family, but we can pray for the strength not to judge them or to be frustrated by their judgment of us, and instead to be able to treat one another with respect and with love.

......ON THE WAY TO MASS

Have you ever said you were sorry? At the beginning of Mass we pray about being sorry. Listen for when we pray, "through my fault, through my fault, / through my most grievous fault." In the Confiteor, we acknowledge our failings and ask the saints and our brothers and sisters to pray for us.

ON THE WAY HOME FROM MASS ......

What is more difficult: to ask for forgiveness for something you have done, or to forgive someone for what they have done to you?

Living the Word

We are Jesus' family, his brothers and sisters. How does he call us to bring peace to our family? How can we practice and live forgiveness and mercy with one another? Pray the Our Father together and discuss what the prayer tells us about God's forgiveness and how we are called to forgive one another.

June 16, 2024

Eleventh Sunday in Ordinary Time

Hearing the Word

Mark 4:26–34

In the name of the Father, and of the Son, and of the Holy Spirit.

Jesus said to the crowds: "This is how it is with the kingdom of God; it is as if a man were to scatter seed on the land and would sleep and rise night and day and through it all the seed would sprout and grow, he knows not how. Of its own accord the land yields fruit, first the blade, then the ear, then the full grain in the ear. And when the grain is ripe, he wields the sickle at once, for the harvest has come."

He said, "To what shall we compare the kingdom of God, or what parable can we use for it? It is like a mustard seed that, when it is sown in the ground, is the smallest of all the seeds on the earth. But once it is sown, it springs up and becomes the largest of plants and puts forth large branches, so that the birds of the sky can dwell in its shade." With many such parables he spoke the word to them as they were able to understand it. Without parables he did not speak to them, but to his own disciples he explained everything in private.

Reflecting on the Word

In the first part of the Gospel, a farmer plants seeds, and while he sleeps, they grow. As parents, we marvel at the growth we see in our children—the new things they learn even without our aid or effort! Although God is the invisible source of their growth, God wants us to participate with him in planting seeds that will bear fruit both in our children's lives and in the kingdom of God. Consider that the power of the Holy Spirit at work in your children is the same Holy Spirit at work in the kingdom of God.

......ON THE WAY TO MASS

What does a seed need to grow? Can we make a seed grow? Whose strength or energy is inside the seed that allows it to grow and change?

ON THE WAY HOME FROM MASS ......

How are we like the mustard seed? We started out very small and hidden. What happened to us? How have we changed? How have we grown? Are we done growing? What are some of the ways we continue to grow?

Living the Word

Take a walk as a family and find the tallest tree you can find in your neighborhood. Think about how it started as a tiny seed and grew bit by bit into this large tree. How is the power of God at work in that seed or tree? How do we measure and track our growth, physically and spiritually?

June 23, 2024

Twelfth Sunday in Ordinary Time

Hearing the Word

Mark 4:35–41

In the name of the Father, and of the Son, and of the Holy Spirit.

On that day, as evening drew on, Jesus said to his disciples: "Let us cross to the other side." Leaving the crowd, they took Jesus with them in the boat just as he was. And other boats were with him. A violent squall came up and waves were breaking over the boat, so that it was already filling up. Jesus was in the stern, asleep on a cushion. They woke him and said to him, "Teacher, do you not care that we are perishing?" He woke up, rebuked the wind, and said to the sea, "Quiet! Be still!" The wind ceased and there was great calm. Then he asked them, "Why are you terrified? Do you not yet have faith?" They were filled with great awe and said to one another, "Who then is this whom even wind and sea obey?"

Reflecting on the Word

Jesus has power over the elements, calming even the violent storm. He teaches his disciples to trust in him, to have faith that he will protect them from harm. The disciples fear the power of the storm, but they forget one essential fact: Jesus is in the boat with them! He never left them alone and is present in the storm with them. We cry out to Jesus in fear, and he appears to be asleep in the boat. But he is awake, looking after our needs. How can we move past doubt and fear to a place of peace and calm? How can we witness this trust to our children?

· · · · · · ON THE WAY TO MASS

Who do you talk to when you are worried or have a concern? How can we share our worries with Jesus at Mass today?

ON THE WAY HOME FROM MASS · · · · · ·

Why were the disciples worried about the storm? Why wasn't Jesus worried about it?

Living the Word

Living in the trust of God's protection brings us peace and calm. How can we trust in God's love and protection? What do we need to release control of, and what worries and concerns can we place in God's hands? As a family, allow each individual family member to talk about any concerns or worries. Then pray the together, asking God to give you peace and calm.

June 30, 2024

Thirteenth Sunday in Ordinary Time

Hearing the Word

Mark 5:22–23, 35–42a

In the name of the Father, and of the Son, and of the Holy Spirit.

One of the synagogue officials, named Jairus, came forward. Seeing him he fell at his feet and pleaded earnestly with him, saying, "My daughter is at the point of death. Please, come lay your hands on her that she may get well and live."

While he was still speaking, people from the synagogue official's house arrived and said, "Your daughter has died; why trouble the teacher any longer?" Disregarding the message that was reported, Jesus said to the synagogue official, "Do not be afraid; just have faith." He did not allow anyone to accompany him inside except Peter, James, and John, the brother of James. When they arrived at the house of the synagogue official, he caught sight of a commotion, people weeping and wailing loudly. So he went in and said to them, "Why this commotion and weeping? The child is not dead but asleep." . . . He took along the child's father and mother and those who were with him and entered the room where the child was. He took the child by the hand and said to her, *"Talitha koum,"* which means, "Little girl, I say to you, arise!" The girl, a child of twelve, arose immediately and walked around.

Reflecting on the Word

Jesus restored the synagogue official's daughter to life. He tells Jairus, "Do not be afraid; just have faith." He encourages us to trust in him. When we experience obstacles in our lives, it can feel like things may never get better, that they will never change. We all need healing. The Bible speaks of spiritual healing, emotional healing, and physical healing. What type of healing do you long for in your life?

• • • • • • ON THE WAY TO MASS

When we are not feeling well, who takes care of us? Do we need anything special when we are sick?

ON THE WAY HOME FROM MASS • • • • • •

Jesus restores the girl back to life. In what ways does the Mass restore us to new life?

Living the Word

Let us pray today for those who care for the sick: nurses, doctors, and professional caregivers. Let us also pray for family and friends who are caring for their loved ones, and for those who are suffering in isolation. Have your children create thank-you cards for a health care worker or get-well cards for someone who is sick.

July 7, 2024

Fourteenth Sunday in Ordinary Time

Hearing the Word

Mark 6:1–6

In the name of the Father, and of the Son, and of the Holy Spirit.

Jesus departed from there and came to his native place, accompanied by his disciples. When the sabbath came he began to teach in the synagogue, and many who heard him were astonished. They said, "Where did this man get all this? What kind of wisdom has been given him? What mighty deeds are wrought by his hands! Is he not the carpenter, the son of Mary, and the brother of James and Joses and Judas and Simon? And are not his sisters here with us?" And they took offense at him. Jesus said to them, "A prophet is not without honor except in his native place and among his own kin and in his own house." So he was not able to perform any mighty deed there, apart from curing a few sick people by laying his hands on them. He was amazed at their lack of faith.

Reflecting on the Word

Jesus returns to his hometown of Nazareth. The young carpenter has become a wonderful speaker, and the people who have known him for their entire lives are astonished by his words and what they heard he had done. He, in turn, is amazed at their lack of faith. How often do we look at someone in our immediate family and limit them to a certain way of being? Let us pray and ask God that each member of our family may grow to become the individual God created them to be, and that we have the grace to recognize their growth and transformation.

......ON THE WAY TO MASS

Have you ever wondered what you will be like when you grow up? What do you think you will become?

ON THE WAY HOME FROM MASS ......

How would you describe Jesus of Nazareth? Who is he for you?

Living the Word

We ask questions as we grow older, such as, "Who am I? Where did I come from? Why am I here? Where am I going?" Where can we find the answers to those questions? Christ helps us— through the Bible and through the gift of the sacraments—to write our own blank page in the history of salvation. Turn off the television, computer, tablet, games, and so on, and open the Bible to the Gospels. Read about the life of Jesus of Nazareth. Allow this time with his Word to help shape us as a family and as individuals, so we can be the person God created us to be.

July 14, 2024

Fifteenth Sunday in Ordinary Time

Hearing the Word

Mark 6:7–13

In the name of the Father, and of the Son, and of the Holy Spirit.

Jesus summoned the Twelve and began to send them out two by two and gave them authority over unclean spirits. He instructed them to take nothing for the journey but a walking stick—no food, no sack, no money in their belts. They were, however, to wear sandals but not a second tunic. He said to them, "Wherever you enter a house, stay there until you leave. Whatever place does not welcome you or listen to you, leave there and shake the dust off your feet in testimony against them." So they went off and preached repentance. The Twelve drove out many demons, and they anointed with oil many who were sick and cured them.

Reflecting on the Word

Jesus summoned the Twelve and began to send them out two by two and gave them authority over unclean spirits. He told them to take nothing for the journey but a walking stick. No extra food, or sack, nor any money. The ministry they have been given must be done in pairs; it must be challenging to accomplish alone. Do you see any correlation between what Jesus is telling the Twelve and the life of your family? How do we support our spouse and our children in their discipleship, as followers of Jesus?

......ON THE WAY TO MASS

The disciples were instructed to take a walking stick for their journey. A walking stick is something that they could lean on for support as they made their way. Who do you lean on for support?

ON THE WAY HOME FROM MASS ......

The disciples went out two by two. Jesus must have known that they would need a friend, a companion to walk with them on this journey. Who walks with you as you follow Jesus? Who are you grateful for today as your "companion in Christ"?

Living the Word

As a family, make a list of the essential items you would pack if you were going on vacation. Now read Mark 6:7–13 and write a second list of all those items that Jesus instructed the Twelve to take with them and compare your two lists. Even with very few material items, the Twelve were able to accomplish so much in the name of Jesus. What is essential for your family as you serve others and share the Good News of Jesus?

July 21, 2024

Sixteenth Sunday in Ordinary Time

Hearing the Word

Mark 6:30–34

In the name of the Father, and of the Son, and of the Holy Spirit.

The apostles gathered together with Jesus and reported all they had done and taught. He said to them, "Come away by yourselves to a deserted place and rest a while." People were coming and going in great numbers, and they had no opportunity even to eat. So they went off in the boat by themselves to a deserted place. People saw them leaving and many came to know about it. They hastened there on foot from all the towns and arrived at the place before them.

When he disembarked and saw the vast crowd, his heart was moved with pity for them, for they were like sheep without a shepherd; and he began to teach them many things.

Reflecting on the Word

The people hastened to be wherever Jesus was. They came in such large numbers that Jesus and the apostles could not even eat and had to retreat to a deserted place, but the people came to them regardless. Instead of turning them away, Jesus, the Good Shepherd, saw their need and taught them. As parents, we often care for the needs of everyone else in our family before our own needs. We know that we (just like Jesus' disciples) must rest, so that we can be our best. It is more difficult when we are tired and cranky to be able to do God's will.

• • • • • • ON THE WAY TO MASS

What are the benefits that come from taking time to rest?
How can time for reflection and prayer bring us closer to Jesus?

ON THE WAY HOME FROM MASS • • • • • •

How is Jesus able to continue to care for people even when he doesn't get much time to rest? Where does his strength come from?

Living the Word

As a family, look at your calendar and all the activities that are marked there. Ask your family if you have built into your schedule the appropriate amount of time for rest and relaxation with the Lord. If not, talk about what a rest and renewal night might look like in your home and see if you can mark one night each week for that time.

July 28, 2024

Seventeenth Sunday in Ordinary Time

Hearing the Word

John 6:5–14

In the name of the Father, and of the Son, and of the Holy Spirit.

When Jesus raised his eyes and saw that a large crowd was coming to him, he said to Philip, "Where can we buy enough food for them to eat?" He said this to test him, because he himself knew what he was going to do. Philip answered him, "Two hundred days' wages worth of food would not be enough for each of them to have a little." One of his disciples, Andrew, the brother of Simon Peter, said to him, "There is a boy here who has five barley loaves and two fish; but what good are these for so many?" Jesus said, "Have the people recline." Now there was a great deal of grass in that place. So the men reclined, about five thousand in number. Then Jesus took the loaves, gave thanks, and distributed them to those who were reclining, and also as much of the fish as they wanted. When they had had their fill, he said to his disciples, "Gather the fragments left over, so that nothing will be wasted." So they collected them, and filled twelve wicker baskets with fragments from the five barley loaves that had been more than they could eat. When the people saw the sign he had done, they said, "This is truly the Prophet, the one who is to come into the world."

Reflecting on the Word

In today's Gospel, Jesus feeds a large group of people with only five barely loaves and two fish. There are many times in our lives as parents when we feel as though we have limited resources to face such great need and demand in the life of our family. Our financial, emotional, or spiritual resources may be depleted. Even when we lack what we need for our family, God is at work. Have you ever experienced an abundance of God's goodness in your poverty? How can we have faith in these trying times?

...... ON THE WAY TO MASS

Today, we hear that a large crowd followed Jesus. Listen for what small amount of food the disciples find, and who it is who shares the food with Jesus.

ON THE WAY HOME FROM MASS ......

What did Jesus do to the food in today's Gospel? How does Jesus feed us today?

Living the Word

Invite family members to make a list of what is needed for the family to be truly happy and healthy. What is essential for the life of our family? Reread the Gospel (John 6:5–14) and discuss how Jesus took care of the needs of the people who came to hear him.

August 4, 2024

Eighteenth Sunday in Ordinary Time

Hearing the Word

John 6:26–35

In the name of the Father, and of the Son, and of the Holy Spirit.

[Jesus said,] "Amen, amen, I say to you, you are looking for me not because you saw signs but because you ate the loaves and were filled. Do not work for food that perishes but for the food that endures for eternal life, which the Son of Man will give you. For on him the Father, God, has set his seal." So they said to him, "What can we do to accomplish the works of God?" Jesus answered and said to them, "This is the work of God, that you believe in the one he sent." So they said to him, "What sign can you do, that we may see and believe in you? What can you do? Our ancestors ate manna in the desert, as it is written: *He gave them bread from heaven to eat.*" So Jesus said to them, "Amen, amen, I say to you, it was not Moses who gave the bread from heaven; my Father gives you the true bread from heaven. For the bread of God is that which comes down from heaven and gives life to the world."

So they said to him, "Sir, give us this bread always." Jesus said to them, "I am the bread of life; whoever comes to me will never hunger, and whoever believes in me will never thirst."

Reflecting on the Word

When we receive Christ in the Eucharist, we are strengthened by his life inside us. In today's Gospel, the people are searching for Jesus and are wanting to see signs confirming that Jesus is the one sent by God. Jesus tells the people that he is the bread sent by God. If they believe and follow Jesus, they will never be hungry again. For what do you hunger? How does the Eucharist we receive at Mass feed you throughout the week?

......ON THE WAY TO MASS

At every Mass, we pray the Our Father. We ask God to "give us this day our daily bread." Is this only about food? What else do we need every day?

ON THE WAY HOME FROM MASS ......

In today's Gospel, Jesus tells us that he is the Bread of Life. He is not just bread for today, but for life. What could that mean for us?

Living the Word

Jesus tells the people that he is the Bread of Life. The people in the Gospel followed him because they thought he could give them the bread they needed to fill their stomachs; they did not understand that he would provide nourishment for their spiritual hunger. Discuss how Jesus satisfies the hungers of our hearts, and how we could not survive if we do not remain with him. Pray the Our Father as a family. Make a prayer card with the words "Give us this day our daily bread."

August 11, 2024

Nineteenth Sunday in Ordinary Time

Hearing the Word

John 6:41–51

In the name of the Father, and of the Son, and of the Holy Spirit.

The Jews murmured about Jesus because he said, "I am the bread that came down from heaven," and they said, "Is this not Jesus, the son of Joseph? Do we not know his father and mother? Then how can he say, 'I have come down from heaven'?" Jesus answered and said to them, "Stop murmuring among yourselves. No one can come to me unless the Father who sent me draw him, and I will raise him on the last day. It is written in the prophets: *They shall all be taught by God.* Everyone who listens to my Father and learns from him comes to me. Not that anyone has seen the Father except the one who is from God; he has seen the Father. Amen, amen, I say to you, whoever believes has eternal life. I am the bread of life. Your ancestors ate the manna in the desert, but they died; this is the bread that comes down from heaven so that one may eat it and not die. I am the living bread that came down from heaven; whoever eats this bread will live forever; and the bread that I will give is my flesh for the life of the world."

Reflecting on the Word

Jesus is the Bread of Life. Why is the Bread of Life an important title for Christ? How does this title help us to more fully realize Jesus' identity and the Eucharistic gift that he offers to us? God the Father is leading us into divine life with him because he loves us unconditionally, with no limits. This is the way that we as parents love our children. Think about how the Eucharist nourishes people of all ages, all cultures, all times, binding us all together.

......ON THE WAY TO MASS

How do you feel when you are hungry? What happens when you do not have something to eat? In today's Mass, we will hear about Jesus being the Bread of Life. How does the Eucharist feed us?

ON THE WAY HOME FROM MASS ......

We have received so much from God. How do we return that love to him?

Living the Word

The Eucharist is the greatest way we receive the gifts of God and the way we give honor and love to God the Father. Take a sheet of paper and draw a line down the middle. On one side, write "Gifts from God at Mass." Then list all the gifts that are present for your family in the liturgy. On the other side, title it "Give God honor, love, and praise." Finally, list all the ways we show God the Father honor, love, and praise at Mass. Which list is longer?

August 15, 2024

Solemnity of the Assumption of the Blessed Virgin Mary

Hearing the Word

Luke 1:46–55

In the name of the Father, and of the Son, and of the Holy Spirit.

And Mary said:

"My soul proclaims the greatness of the Lord; / my spirit rejoices in God my Savior / for he has looked with favor upon his lowly servant. / From this day all generations will call me blessed: / the Almighty has done great things for me / and holy is his Name. / He has mercy on those who fear him / in every generation. / He has shown the strength of his arm, / and has scattered the proud in their conceit. / He has cast down the mighty from their thrones, / and has lifted up the lowly. / He has filled the hungry with good things, / and the rich he has sent away empty. / He has come to the help of his servant Israel / for he has remembered his promise of mercy, / the promise he made to our fathers, / to Abraham and his children forever."

Reflecting on the Word

Today, we will hear some beautiful words from Mary. This prayer is called the Magnificat. It is also known as the Song of Mary or the Canticle of Mary. Mary thanks God for all her blessings. She then goes on to tell us about God: God cares for the poor, the hungry, and those who are weak and vulnerable. Mary rejoices for all the ways that God has been present in her life. How do you recognize and rejoice with how God is in your own life? How often do you praise him in your prayer?

......ON THE WAY TO MASS

This week's Gospel features the Magnificat, Mary's prayer of praise. At Mass, listen for moments when we praise the Lord. How do we praise him?

ON THE WAY HOME FROM MASS ......

The Magnificat speaks of God's mercy and his faithfulness to his Chosen People through the generations. Through our baptism, we have become part of God's holy people. How has God shown us his mercy? What promise has he made to us? How has he protected us?

Living the Word

Mary's prayer focuses on her joy and her gratitude to the Lord. As a family, write a prayer that expresses your joy and thanks to God. Once the prayer is written, make this prayer a part of your family ritual. Make a prayer card for the prayer table or write the words and post it on the fridge or the bathroom mirror or a place where everyone will see it and recite it each day.

August 18, 2024

Twentieth Sunday in Ordinary Time

Hearing the Word

John 6:51–58

In the name of the Father, and of the Son, and of the Holy Spirit.

Jesus said to the crowds: "I am the living bread that came down from heaven; whoever eats this bread will live forever; and the bread that I will give is my flesh for the life of the world."

The Jews quarreled among themselves, saying, "How can this man give us his flesh to eat?" Jesus said to them, "Amen, amen, I say to you, unless you eat the flesh of the Son of Man and drink his blood, you do not have life within you. Whoever eats my flesh and drinks my blood has eternal life, and I will raise him on the last day. For my flesh is true food, and my blood is true drink. Whoever eats my flesh and drinks my blood remains in me and I in him. Just as the living Father sent me and I have life because of the Father, so also the one who feeds on me will have life because of me. This is the bread that came down from heaven. Unlike your ancestors who ate and still died, whoever eats this bread will live forever."

Reflecting on the Word

Jesus gives us an incredible gift. He gives us his Body and Blood for us to share in his eternal life. We become brothers and sisters with Christ and with our community of faith because of this shared life. The Eucharist is not simply a representation or reenactment of this Gospel—it is truly his Body and Blood, broken and shared today.

· · · · · · ON THE WAY TO MASS

Each time we go to Mass, we participate in a meal with Jesus. He did not give us his Body and Blood only once. He continues to give it to us at every Mass. How can we thank him for this gift?

ON THE WAY HOME FROM MASS · · · · · ·

What does it mean when Jesus said, "Whoever eats this bread will live forever"? How does he nourish us—through his Word, sacraments, and prayer?

Living the Word

We have received the gift of eternal life through the Eucharist. While this is a personal gift for each of us, it is also a calling to invite others to eternal life in the kingdom of heaven. Jesus said, "Whoever eats my flesh and drinks my blood remains in me and I in him." How are our lives affected by our remaining in him and he in us? Imagine what the world might be like today if all people respected and valued the Eucharist. Draw a picture of what the world might look like if we showed our love for the Eucharist. Share these pictures with your parish priest.

August 25, 2024

Twenty-first Sunday in Ordinary Time

Hearing the Word

John 6:60–69

In the name of the Father, and of the Son, and of the Holy Spirit.

Many of Jesus' disciples who were listening said, "This saying is hard; who can accept it?" Since Jesus knew that his disciples were murmuring about this, he said to them, "Does this shock you? What if you were to see the Son of Man ascending to where he was before? It is the spirit that gives life, while the flesh is of no avail. The words I have spoken to you are Spirit and life. But there are some of you who do not believe." Jesus knew from the beginning the ones who would not believe and the one who would betray him. And he said, "For this reason I have told you that no one can come to me unless it is granted him by my Father."

As a result of this, many of his disciples returned to their former way of life and no longer accompanied him. Jesus then said to the Twelve, "Do you also want to leave?" Simon Peter answered him, "Master, to whom shall we go? You have the words of eternal life. We have come to believe and are convinced that you are the Holy One of God."

Reflecting on the Word

Jesus asks his friends, "Do you also want to leave?" Like Simon Peter, we want to respond, "Lord, to whom shall we go? You have the words of eternal life." We see people in our community, our workplace, and sometimes in our own family who walk away from Jesus. There are days we have doubts and may feel that we have walked away in some sense. Let us ask Jesus to help us to draw closer to him.

......ON THE WAY TO MASS

At Mass, the priest makes a gesture over the bread and the wine, asking God to send down the Holy Spirit. This gesture starts up high and ends down low. Watch for this moment during the Liturgy of the Eucharist.

ON THE WAY HOME FROM MASS ......

Where did you see the gesture calling down the Holy Spirit? Why do we invoke the Holy Spirit at this moment in the Mass? It is the Spirit who changes the bread and wine into the Body and Blood of Jesus, and it is the Spirit who gives us faith to believe in his real presence!

Living the Word

While Jesus' teachings are indeed hard, we are called as a people of faith to live out these teachings. This is not something that we do alone, as the Holy Spirit is always with us, guiding us toward the kingdom of heaven. What moments have you seen the Holy Spirit working in your life? Write a prayer to the Holy Spirit or draw an image of the Holy Spirit at work in your life.

September 1, 2024

Twenty-second Sunday in Ordinary Time

Hearing the Word

Mark 7:5–8, 14–15, 21–23

In the name of the Father, and of the Son, and of the Holy Spirit.

[The] Pharisees and scribes questioned [Jesus], "Why do your disciples not follow the tradition of the elders but instead eat a meal with unclean hands?" He responded, "Well did Isaiah prophesy about you hypocrites, as it is written: / *This people honors me with their lips, / but their hearts are far from me; / in vain do they worship me, / teaching as doctrines human precepts.* / You disregard God's commandment but cling to human tradition."

He summoned the crowd again and said to them, "Hear me, all of you, and understand. Nothing that enters one from outside can defile that person; but the things that come out from within are what defile.

"From within people, from their hearts, come evil thoughts, unchastity, theft, murder, adultery, greed, malice, deceit, licentiousness, envy, blasphemy, arrogance, folly. All these evils come from within and they defile."

Reflecting on the Word

The Pharisees were caught up in the form of the law (how people obey it) but had forgotten about the spirit of the law (why people obey it). Without the spirit of the law, there is no connection to the law's purpose. Jesus reminds us that the reason we obey God's commandments is to draw closer to God. Mass is an opportunity to spend time with and celebrate with God our Father, but it is possible to go through the motions while our hearts remain far from him. In what ways can we bring our hearts closer to God? What would that look like for your family?

......ON THE WAY TO MASS

Do you follow rules and laws at home, at school, traffic laws, and so on? What would happen if we did not have rules?

ON THE WAY HOME FROM MASS ......

God has established commandments for his people. Why did God establish these commandments? Who were they created for? Why are they important? Why do we follow them?

Living the Word

Every family has rules to follow. It is easy to judge our brothers and sisters, our classmates, and our friends when they break a rule or feel upset that they do not have to live by the same rules we do. Discuss the important rules in your home, and how you make peace with one another. Discuss how we can make room for peace at home. Where do we experience peace? Who is the source of all peace?

EVERYDAY FAMILY PRAYERS

The Sign of the Cross

The sign of the cross is the first prayer and the last—of each day, and of each Christian life. It is a prayer of the body as well as a prayer of words. When we are presented for baptism, the community traces this sign on our bodies for the first time. Parents may trace it daily on their children. We learn to trace it daily on ourselves and on those whom we love. When we die, our loved ones will trace this holy sign on us for the last time.

In the name of the Father,

and of the Son,

and of the Holy Spirit. Amen.

The Lord's Prayer

The Lord's Prayer, or the Our Father, is a very important prayer for Christians because Jesus himself taught it to his disciples, who taught it to his Church. Today, we say this prayer as part of Mass, in the Rosary, and in personal prayer. There are seven petitions in the Lord's Prayer. The first three ask for God to be glorified and praised, and the next four ask for God to help take care of our physical and spiritual needs.

Our Father, who art in heaven,

hallowed be thy name;

thy kingdom come,

thy will be done

on earth as it is in heaven.

Give us this day our daily bread,

and forgive us our trespasses,

as we forgive those who trespass against us;

and lead us not into temptation, but deliver us from evil.

The Apostles' Creed

The Apostles' Creed is one of the earliest creeds we have; scholars believe it was written in the second century. The Apostles' Creed is shorter than the Nicene Creed, but it states what we believe about the Father, Son, and Holy Spirit. This prayer is sometimes used at Mass, especially at Masses with children, and is part of the Rosary.

I believe in God,

the Father almighty,

Creator of heaven and earth,

and in Jesus Christ, his only Son, our Lord,

who was conceived by the Holy Spirit,

born of the Virgin Mary,

suffered under Pontius Pilate,

was crucified, died and was buried;

he descended into hell;

and on the third day he rose again from the dead;

he ascended into heaven,

and is seated at the right hand of God the Father almighty;

from there he will come to judge the living and the dead.

I believe in the Holy Spirit,

the holy catholic Church,

the communion of saints,

the forgiveness of sins,

the resurrection of the body,

and life everlasting. Amen.

The Nicene Creed

The Nicene Creed was written at the Council of Nicaea in AD 325, when bishops of the Church gathered together in order to articulate true belief in who Christ is and in his relationship to God the Father. The Nicene Creed was the final document of that Council, written so that all the faithful may know the central teachings of Christianity. We say this prayer at Mass.

I believe in one God,

the Father almighty,

maker of heaven and earth,

of all things visible and invisible.

I believe in one Lord Jesus Christ,

the Only Begotten Son of God,

born of the Father before all ages.

God from God, Light from Light,

true God from true God,

begotten, not made, consubstantial with the Father;

through him all things were made.

For us men and for our salvation

he came down from heaven,

and by the Holy Spirit was incarnate of the Virgin Mary,

and became man.

For our sake he was crucified under Pontius Pilate,
he suffered death and was buried,
and rose again on the third day
in accordance with the Scriptures.
He ascended into heaven
and is seated at the right hand of the Father.
He will come again in glory
to judge the living and the dead
and his kingdom will have no end.

I believe in the Holy Spirit, the Lord, the giver of life,
who proceeds from the Father and the Son,
who with the Father and Son is adored and glorified,
who has spoken through the prophets.

I believe in one holy, catholic, and apostolic Church.
I confess one Baptism for the forgiveness of sins
and I look forward to the resurrection of the dead
and the life of the world to come. Amen.

Glory Be (Doxology)

This is a short prayer that Christians sometimes add to the end of psalms. It is prayed during the Rosary and usually follows the opening verse during the Liturgy of the Hours. It can be prayed at any time during the day.

Glory be to the Father

and to the Son

and to the Holy Spirit,

as it was in the beginning

is now, and ever shall be

world without end. Amen.

Hail Mary

The first two lines of this prayer are the words of the angel Gabriel to Mary, when he announces that she is with child (Luke 1:28). The second two lines are Elizabeth's greeting to Mary (Luke 1:42). The last four lines come to us from deep in history, from where and from whom we do not know. This prayer is part of the Rosary and is often used by Christians for personal prayer.

Hail, Mary, full of grace,

the Lord is with thee.

Blessed art thou among women

and blessed is the fruit of thy womb, Jesus.

Holy Mary, Mother of God,

pray for us sinners,

now and at the hour of our death.

Amen.

Grace before Meals

Families pray before meals in different ways. Some families make up a prayer in their own words, other families sing a prayer, and many families use this traditional formula. Teach your children to say this prayer while signing themselves with the cross.

Bless us, O Lord, and these thy gifts,

which we are about to receive from thy bounty,

through Christ our Lord.

Amen.

Grace after Meals

Teach your children to say this prayer after meals, while signing themselves with the cross. The part in brackets is optional.

We give thee thanks, for all thy benefits,

almighty God, who lives and reigns forever.

[And may the souls of the faithful departed,

through the mercy of God, rest in peace.]

Amen.

About the Author

Mary Heinrich is a catechist and formation leader for the Catechesis of the Good Shepherd method of faith formation for children. She is the membership coordinator for Catechesis of the Good Shepherd USA (CGSUSA). She has served as a parish catechetical leader for twenty-nine years, as well as a consultant for religious education publishers. Mary earned a BA in theology from Mount Mercy College in Cedar Rapids, Iowa, and a MA in pastoral studies (MAPS-CGS) from the Aquinas Institute of Theology in St. Louis, Missouri. She is married to Kurt, a deacon for the Diocese of Des Moines, and they are parents to daughter, Clare.